Blue and White
Transfer Ware 1780-1840

BLUE AND WHITE TRANSFER WARE
1780-1840

A. W. Coysh

DAVID & CHARLES
Newton Abbot   London

British Library Cataloguing in Publication Data

Coysh, A. W.
   Blue and white transfer ware 1780–1840.
   1. Pottery, English   2. Blue and white transfer
  ware
  I. Title
  738.3'7   NK4085

  ISBN 0-7153-6535-5

First published 1970
Second revised edition 1974
Second impression 1979
Third impression 1982

© A. W. COYSH 1970, 1974

Printed in Great Britain
by Biddles Limited Guildford
for David & Charles (Publishers) Limited
Brunel House Newton Abbot Devon

CONTENTS

Acknowledgements 6

Transfer-printed Wares in Underglaze Blue 7

The Years of Experiment 10

Expansion and Decline 20

Problems of Attribution 96

Notes for the Collector 110

Index 112

ACKNOWLEDGEMENTS

Many people have helped me while I have been compiling this book on the patterns to be found on blue and white transfer ware. My greatest debt is to Mr Richard Clements who took most of the photographs and prepared the layout for the illustrations. In addition, he has spent much time ferreting in antique shops and markets with great success in the search for marked specimens. Those who have allowed me to photograph pieces in their possession are acknowledged in the captions.

It would be impossible to list everyone with whom I have discussed these wares. Among those I have to thank are Mr and Mrs David Aliband; Mr J. Bromley of the Guildhall Library, London; the Hon Mrs J. Bruce; Mrs Elizabeth Carter; Mr T. R. Copeland; Mr R. H. Coysh; Miss M. A. Gill of the Laing Art Gallery and Museum, Newcastle-upon-Tyne; Mr G. A. Godden; Mr and Mrs A. de Saye Hutton; Mr and Mrs John May; Mr A. R. Mountford who allowed me to burrow in the basement of the City Museum of Stoke-on-Trent; Mr W. N. Nichols of the Salters' Company; Mr H. Norwood of the Hampshire County Museum Service; Mr Michael Robinson of Rotherham Museum; Mr and Mrs Graham Salmon; Mr Alan Smith of the City of Liverpool Museums; Mr Morris Tucker and Mr Len Whiter.

NOTE TO SECOND EDITION

Many collectors in Britain and America have kindly written to me with new information about makers and patterns mentioned in this book. Some of these facts have been incorporated in my second book, *Blue and White Earthenware, 1800–1850* but it has also been possible to add new material to this revised edition. I am grateful to members of the Friends of Blue Club, in particular to Mr Robin Gurnett, Dr Richard Henrywood and Mr W. L. Little whose enthusiasm knows no bounds.

A. W. COYSH

By the same author

The Antique Buyer's Dictionary of Names
Blue-Printed Earthenware, 1800–1850

TRANSFER-PRINTED WARES IN UNDERGLAZE BLUE

In 1780 the first earthenwares to be transfer-printed in blue and then glazed were made by Thomas Turner at Caughley in Shropshire. The new style of decoration had a profound effect on the pottery industry. By the end of the eighteenth century similar wares were being produced in Staffordshire, Lancashire, Yorkshire and South Wales. The first twenty years were largely experimental and most of the patterns were derived from designs on Chinese ceramics.

Early in the nineteenth century great advances were made. As a result of the invention of the Fourdrinier paper-making machine a more suitable transfer paper became available which enabled the engravers to do finer work, combining stipple with line engraving. Designs were no longer solely from the Chinese; scenes appeared which were based on engravings in books on India and the Ottoman Empire, and so did rural scenes with historic houses, abbeys and castles. Many of the plates and dishes had borders of garden flowers, echoing contemporary designs on fabrics and wallpapers. An export trade in blue-printed wares grew rapidly, especially after the Napoleonic Wars. North America was the main market and many potters sent shiploads of their blue-printed wares across the Atlantic, many decorated with American scenes. They were distributed through agents or even auctioned on the dockside in such ports as Montreal, Boston, New York, Philadelphia and New Orleans. The trade flourished for about fifteen years but declined in the 1830s with the production of new types of earthenware and the expansion of American potteries.

The blue-printed wares produced between about 1805 and 1825 are often of superb quality, fine products of co-operative craftsmanship and practical skill. They are collected on both sides of the Atlantic and those originally intended for the home market in Britain have now become exports to America as 'antiques'. The serious collector has therefore a wide field for study and must first understand how the wares were produced.

The Technical Process

The first stage in the production of blue-printed wares was the engraving of copper plates. Since dinner services made up the bulk of the output this involved a whole series of engravings to produce prints to fit plates, dishes, tureens, sauceboats, jugs and strainers. Some firms employed their own engravers but there were also a number of outside engravers who sold copper plates to any potter who required them. The plates were engraved more deeply than for book illustrations, particularly in the early days when paper was rather coarse. The porous biscuit absorbed more of the ink. Cobalt blue was used for the printing because it was the only colour at that time which could withstand the heat of the glost oven without blurring.

The cobalt blue was mainly imported from Germany. The ore of cobalt when roasted produced *zaffre* which, when fused with sand and potassium carbonate gave a blue glassy *smalt* containing a dark-blue crystalline cobalt compound. Supplies of cobalt were interrupted during the Napoleonic Wars and the necessary materials were obtained from Cornwall. The cobalt compound was mixed with powdered flint and oil into a viscous ink for printing. The copper plates were first warmed on a stove and the ink was spread over the metal with a palette knife and worked into the details of the engraving. The surface was then scraped and cleaned with a pad of corduroy. The transfer paper was made wet with soap and water and laid on the copper plate. Pressure was applied and the plate was again warmed on the stove so that the paper could be peeled off with an impression of the engraved pattern.

The transfer of the pattern to the earthenware biscuit was a job for women. A girl 'cutter' trimmed away unwanted paper and a 'transferrer' then placed the paper, ink-side downwards, on the ware, rubbing it gently with a roll of flannel. (The border was applied separately, usually in two or more pieces, and the 'joins' may often be detected.) By washing in cold water immediately afterwards, the paper floated off leaving the inked pattern on the ware. This print was then 'fixed' by heating the ware in a muffle oven.

The final stage involved covering the pattern with a protective glaze. A 'dipper' carefully immersed each piece in the liquid glaze, so that little surplus remained to drain off. This was fixed by heating in a glost oven. Early glazes show a rippled surface and are blue in colour. This colour can be seen very clearly if a plate or dish has a foot rim. By about 1830, however, most glazes were smooth and colourless.

Nomenclature

Unfortunately, the collector will find that few of these blue-printed wares bear the name of the maker. Nevertheless, dealers and auctioneers often attribute pieces to well-known makers or potteries and label them 'Davenport', 'Leeds', 'Liverpool', 'Rogers' or 'Spode' without the slightest evidence to support their attributions. It is immensely difficult to attribute unmarked blue-printed wares with accuracy since there were no copyright laws, and designs were pirated freely. This book illustrates over 140 marked pieces which have appeared in shops or auction sales since 1965 and discusses the attribution of a number of others though it is seldom possible to be certain of the maker of an unmarked piece. One is lucky if one can say 'possibly', and very lucky if one can say 'probably' or 'almost certainly'. To attempt an attribution it is essential to examine every detail. For this reason each illustration has been given a detailed caption with information about foot rims, marks, glazes, etc. One potter, for example, coloured the foot rims of his wares—a useful point to know.

The terms used in describing a dinner plate are shown in the diagram. The surface of the plate or dish which carries the pattern, including the border, is referred to as the 'face'. This is made up of the 'well' which normally carries the main picture, and the 'rim' which normally carries the border pattern. Many plates have an indented edge to the rim; unless this is stated it may be assumed that the edge is smooth and round.

The base of an early plate seldom has a foot rim; where foot rims are present they may be described as 'single', 'double' or 'rounded'. The stilt marks, sometimes called 'cockspur' or 'spur' marks, where the little pyramids of burnt clay which separated plates from their neighbours in the kiln have left a mark on the glaze, sometimes occur as single marks, sometimes in threes or even as short lines. These are referred to where it seems relevant as 'single', 'triple' or 'elongated'.

Colours are difficult to describe. A five-fold range of colours has been used: dark, dark-medium, medium, light-medium and light. All blue-printing, including printed marks, is underglaze.

Border patterns are often clearly defined by continuous narrow bands with geometric motifs. These are referred to as 'stringing', a term borrowed from a description of inlay in furniture. Where patterns have already been given titles, either by the maker

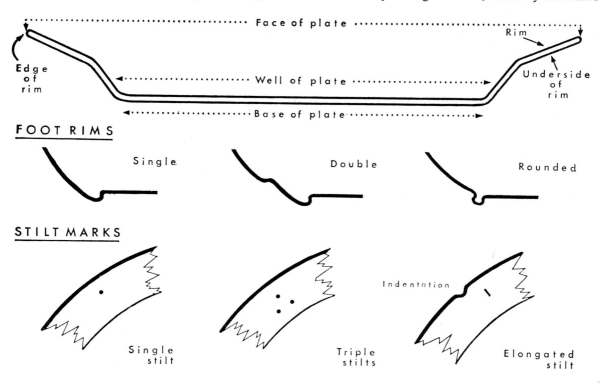

or a previous writer, these are quoted in the captions in inverted commas. In other cases working titles have been adopted and these are indicated by an 'A' in brackets after the name in the caption. Sometimes several potters used different designs with the same title. In such cases it is necessary to refer to them, for example, as 'Spode's *Woodman Pattern*' and 'Rockingham's *Woodman Pattern*'.

References

The literature on blue-printed transfer ware is limited. Frequent reference will, however, be made to the following publications. The author's name only will be used, followed by the number of the page or plate.

Coysh, A. W. *Blue-Printed Earthenware 1800–1850* (1972)

Fontaines, J. K. des. 'Underglaze Blue-printed Earthenware with Particular Reference to Spode', *Transactions of the English Ceramic Circle*, 7 Part 2 (1969)

Godden, G. A. *Encyclopaedia of British Pottery and Porcelain Marks* (1964) (abbreviated to GM followed by the number of the ceramic mark)

Godden, G. A. *An Illustrated Encyclopaedia of British Pottery and Porcelain* (1966) (abbreviated to GI followed by the number of the plate)

Hillier, B. *The Turners of Lane End* (1965)

Laidacker, S. *Anglo-American China*. Parts I and II (Bristol, Pennsylvania, 1951)

Moore, N. H. *The Old China Book* (1935 edition)

Little, W. L. *Staffordshire Blue* (1969)

Turner, W. *Transfer Printing on Enamels, Porcelain and Pottery* (1907)

Whiter, L. *Spode* (1970)

Williams, S. B. *Antique Blue and White Spode* (1949 edition)

Other useful reference books include:

Adams, P. W. L. *A History of the Adams Family of North Staffordshire* (1914)

Barber, E. A. *Anglo-American Pottery* (Indianapolis 1899; Philadelphia 1901)

Camehl, A. W. *The Blue China Book* (New York 1916; 1970)

Eaglestone, A. A. and Lockett, T. A. *The Rockingham Pottery* (Rotherham 1964; 1972)

Earle, A. M. *China Collecting in America* (1892)

Falkner, F. *The Wood Family of Burslem* (1912)

Gatty, C. F. *The Liverpool Potteries* (Liverpool 1882)

Godden, G. A. *Minton Pottery and Porcelain of the First Period, 1793–1850* (1968)

Grabham, O. *Yorkshire Potteries, Pots and Potters* (1916; 1971)

Haggar, R. G. *The Masons of Lane Delph* (1952)

Hayden, A. *Chats on English Earthenware* (1909; 1922); *Spode and his Successors* (1925)

Hughes, G. B. *English and Scottish Earthenware* (1961); *Victorian Pottery and Porcelain* (1959; 1968)

Jewitt, A. *The Ceramic Art of Great Britain* (1878)

Kidson, J. R. and F. *Historical Notices of the Leeds Old Pottery* (1892; 1970)

Lancaster, H. B. *Liverpool and her Potters* (1936)

Larsen, E. B. *American Historical Views on Staffordshire China* (New York, 1939)

Lockett, T. A. *Davenport Pottery and Porcelain* (1972)

Nance, E. M. *The Pottery and Porcelain of Swansea and Nantgarw* (1942)

Nicholls, R. *The Adams Family* (1928)

Peel, D. *A Pride of Potters* (1957)

Pountney, W. J. *Old Bristol Potteries* (1920; 1972)

Rackham, B. *Leeds Pottery* (1938)

Rhead, G. W. *British Pottery Marks* (1910); *The Earthenware Collector* (1920)

Rhead, G. W. and F. A. *Staffordshire Pots and Potters* (1906)

Shaw, S. *A History of the Staffordshire Potteries* (1829; 1970)

Smith, A. *Illustrated Guide to Liverpool Herculaneum Pottery* (1970)

Towner, D. C. *The Leeds Pottery* (1963)

Turner, W. *William Adams, an old English Potter* (1904; 1923)

THE YEARS OF EXPERIMENT

Early patterns

The earliest pattern to be printed in underglaze blue on earthenware (1) was produced at Caughley in 1780. It is not possible to say where the illustrated example was made since it has only a printed six-pointed star as a mark and it is known that a number of other potters copied the design. Nevertheless, the steely-blue colour of this specimen is characteristic of the Caughley Pottery. Copper plates of this design still exist with the initials T.T. (Thomas Turner) engraved in the margin. Thomas Minton, who was an apprentice engraver at Caughley, is often credited with having produced the design. Since it carries a willow tree it may justifiably be described as the first *Willow Pattern* on earthenware. It is important to remember that many engravings were needed to transfer-print on a dinner service. A number of engravers, including Thomas Minton, may therefore have worked with this design. Variants of this pattern with the Caughley C-shaped open crescent mark are illustrated by Little (plate 2) and by Turner (fig A 24). The first maker to use this pattern in Staffordshire was Josiah Spode c1783 (J. K. des Fontaines, plate 140b).

The *Buffalo Pattern* (2) is another early example though no clear indication has been found to establish that it was used at Caughley. The star-shaped mark, however, is identical with that on the willow plate (1). This may only be a printer's piece-work tally but it seems likely that these plates were made in the same pottery. The design was used by several potters in the 1780s and 1790s including Thomas Wolfe (see G. Woolliscroft Rhead, *British Pottery Marks* [1910] p291), Josiah Spode (Williams, fig 96) and Joshua Heath (Little, plates 31 and 32).

The Enterprise of Joshua Heath

Many authors have written of Josiah Spode, John Turner, John Yates and William Adams as pioneers in the field of transfer-printing in underglaze blue but few have given credit to Joshua Heath who produced earthenwares and creamwares between about 1770 and 1800 and was certainly producing blue-printed wares during his later years at Hanley in Staffordshire. According to Godden (GM 1991) he used the impressed Mark IH on wares produced between c1780 and 1800 and many printed pieces bear this mark (3, 4, 5 and 8).

1 (*above left*) *The 'Caughley Willow Pattern'*
Dished indented plate (c1780) printed in a dark, steely blue. The pattern shows a bridge with three arches and a large pagoda within a partially fenced compound. One man stands on the bridge, one man is seated in a boat, and two men stand talking within an unprinted inset. There is a willow tree in the distance beyond the bridge. A cellular printed band frames the picture within the well of the plate.
The rim border repeats the cellular motif with other geometrical designs, small inset scenes, flowers and insects.
Printed mark: small six-pointed star.
Diam 9.7in. No foot rim. Three single stilt marks on base. Blue glaze unevenly applied.

2 (*above right*) *The 'Buffalo Pattern'*
Dished indented plate (c1780–90) with Buffalo pattern in dark, steely blue showing a man with raised left hand mounted on a buffalo. Before him stand a man and a boy, the boy holding a branch. There is also a pagoda; the top storey forms a covered area with open sides in which a figure stands. The picture is framed by a printed band.
The rim border bears the same geometrical pattern but also has an insect motif.
Printed mark: small six-pointed star.
Diam 7.5in. Single foot rim. Three single stilt marks. Creamy body with pale greenish-blue glaze.

3 (*below*) *Joshua Heath's version of the 'Caughley Willow Pattern'*
(Hampshire County Museum Service. No 182 in the Bignell Collection Catalogue, 1943)
Oval dish (c1790) printed in dark blue with a pattern based on the Caughley Willow (1). Note the introduction of Chinese writing scrolls into the border.
Impressed mark: I H.
Length 12.9in. Width 9.3in. No foot rim. White body with bluish rippled glaze.

Joshua Heath must have had a considerable output and he appears to have been very enterprising. He copied the *Caughley Willow Pattern* (see 3) but introduced the Chinese writing scroll into the border, and he used the *Buffalo Pattern* (Little, plates 31 and 32).

Heath also produced designs which have not been seen elsewhere. The long, narrow dish (4), presumably made for serving fish, is remarkable. Not only has it an unusual shape but it carries a most original 'primitive' design which one feels might almost have been drawn by a child. The designer (who may also have been the engraver) has evidently had a completely free hand and although the chinoiserie features which include the usual pagodas, trees and border design are derivative, there are other features such as the seal and the reindeer which are quite out of place in the setting. Everything about the dish suggests experiment. The line engraving is crude, the inking and transfer work amateurish, and the dish seems to have been supported in the glost oven by its rim where the glaze is broken in several places. Yet it is a very attractive dish.

The larger dish (5) has both quality and attraction. The design is more formal but in this case there is a curious blend of Oriental and European. The pagoda rises from behind a wall of rectangular blocks which is broken by a portico more suited to a Georgian city. It is also obvious that the designer had a liking for curves which reveal themselves in the branches of the tree, the gondola-like sampans and the pagoda roof which would look well on a cartoon of Napoleon. The body of this dish could almost be described as creamware.

It is sometimes said that the makers of blue and white transfer pottery liked to cover the surfaces of their wares with all-over patterns to hide imperfections in the body. This is certainly not true of Heath's work. Imperfections exist but they are not obvious and the general appearance of his pieces is nicely balanced and pleasing. Indeed, at first glance, it is difficult to believe that his wares were made in the eighteenth century.

4 (*above*) *Joshua Heath*
Reindeer and Seal Pattern (A)
Long narrow fish dish (c1790) with a willow-type design combining Chinese and arctic features. There is a seal in the foreground and a bridled reindeer held by a man in a conical hat with a feather. Another figure carries a bundle on a stick. To the left is a six-storey pagoda and a group of houses almost immersed in 'windfall apples'. Two birds of unknown species adorn the scene and there are two boats being sculled along in a different perspective. The picture is framed in a dagger band and the rim border has alternate geometrical and insect motifs.
Impressed mark: I H *in rectangle.*
Length 16.8in. Width 8.2in. No foot rim. No stilt marks. Rippled blue glaze on white body.

5 (*below*) *Joshua Heath*
Palladian Pagoda Pattern (A)
Large indented dish (c1790) with chinoiserie including a willow tree in the foreground. The main feature is a pagoda-like building entered through a Palladian pillared portico. Two boats are to be seen: one with three figures seated beneath an umbrella or sunshade, the other with a built canopy with two men—one standing, one seated. The picture is framed by an interlaced band broken in four places by a darker blue motif which matches the rim border. The geometrical design of the rim border is broken by alternate motifs of insects and linked circles.
Impressed mark: I H *in rectangle.*
Length 18.5in. Width 14.5in. No foot rim. Three single stilt marks on base. Clear rippled glaze on a cream-coloured body which contains minute black specks.

Early wares marked 'TURNER'

Two pieces are illustrated—a plate (6) and a dish (7), both of which bear the impressed mark 'TURNER'. They are clearly eighteenth-century examples of transfer printing with line engraving and they are printed in dark blue. Thomas Turner of Caughley used this mark (GM 808) but it is rare and was used before 1780. The mark was also used by John Turner of Lane End, Longton, in Staffordshire (and later by his sons), between 1780 and 1806 (GM 3896). Several features are reminiscent of the early Caughley willow pattern—the 'inset' with figures, for example. In this case, however, there is a printed background as though a wall of the pagoda had been removed to reveal pillars within. It is known, however, that the early Caughley wares were widely copied. The impressed mark is associated with impressed numbers, a feature of John Turner's marks. Another plate, similar to 6, has been noted with a single shallow foot rim. Weighing the evidence, it seems fair to say that these pieces are 'probably John Turner'.

Chinese Patterns

The term 'willow pattern' is commonly applied to a whole range of wares with chinoiserie patterns, often quite wrongly. There are hundreds of patterns which have a willow tree but in many of them (eg 4 and 5) it is not a prominent feature. The standard willow pattern which was being used by many makers in the 1830s has a pagoda, a three-arch bridge, two birds in the sky and a prominent willow tree (see 50 and 109). No chinoiserie design is described in this book as a willow pattern unless it has a prominent willow tree. The Joshua Heath example (8) has a bridge but no recognisable willow tree. The Turner plate (9), however, can be regarded as a true willow pattern though there are only two men on the bridge. This is probably much later than the examples of chinoiserie patterns shown on page 17.

A similar example is illustrated by Hillier (plate 24b) which bears the mark of James Underhill Mist, Turner's London agent, who operated from 82 Fleet Street. This dates it to the 1811–14 period, when William Turner, John Turner's son, was running the works, though it could have been introduced before this. However, it is in a medium blue and Turner's early productions were printed in a darker blue. Hillier illustrates what appears to have been an earlier pattern (plate 24a) which has an elephant with a twisted trunk, and is said to be one of a

6 (above left) Probably John Turner
The Stag Pattern (A)
(Courtesy: Mr and Mrs A. de Saye Hutton)
Indented plate (c1785–90), in dark, steely blue, with a picture of a running stag pursued by a man and a dog. The 'inset' in a pagoda shows a pillared interior with a man, as though an oval piece has been cut from the pagoda wall. There are two small boats with pennants on the water. The border has a geometrical design with a cellular motif.
Impressed mark: TURNER.
Diam 8.0in. No foot rim. Rippled blue glaze.

7 (above right) Probably John Turner
The Stag Pattern (A)
Dish (c1785–90), roughly triangular in shape, with rounded indented corners, with a printed pattern similar to 6.

O

Impressed mark: TURNER.

I

Distance from base of triangle to apex 10.1in. The rim of the dish stands 1.9in above the base. No foot rim. Blue glaze unevenly applied.

8 (below left) Joshua Heath
Conversation Pattern (A)
Indented plate (c1795–1800) in dark blue, with chinoiserie including pagodas and several 'apple' trees. Two men stand face-to-face in conversation on a single-arch bridge. The boat in the foreground carries a pennant. An inner band of geometrical and floral motifs frames the picture. The rim border is similar.

3

Impressed mark: I H.
Diam 9.5in. Single foot rim. Bluish rippled glaze on creamware body.

9 (below right) John Turner
Two-man Willow Pattern (A)
Stoneware indented plate (c1810–12), in medium blue, with a willow pattern. The bridge has a single arch (with a 'spotted' portion) on which two men are walking, one carrying a crook, the other a large writing scroll. 'Apple' trees of two types appear. The picture is framed by stringing of catherine-wheel scrolls. The border pattern has geometrical motifs including a cellular design with scrolls, leaves and flowers.
Impressed mark: TURNER.
Diam 9.1in. Double unglazed foot rim. No stilt marks. Pale blue glaze on bluish stoneware body.

series which included deer, gazelle and rhinoceros designs. It seems likely that there was also an earlier willow pattern, possibly designed by William Underwood, a blue-printer from Worcester, who came to work for Turner before 1787 (Shaw, S., *History of The Staffordshire Potteries* [1829] p214).

The Turner *Two-man Willow Pattern* (9) was used by G. M. and C. J. Mason of Lane Delph, Staffordshire, between c1813 and 1835, also on stoneware, with the MASON'S PATENT IRON-STONE CHINA mark (GM 2539) impressed in one line. The patterns are identical; it is possible that Mason's acquired the copper plates some time after 1813, or they may have decided to copy a pattern which they knew had gone out of use.

The plates with chinoiserie (10, 11 and 12) show how difficult it can be to attribute patterns to factories when a maker's name is not present. The pattern used by the Cambrian Pottery at Swansea (10) and by the Leeds Pottery (12) have very similar borders with Chinese writing scrolls. The main difference is that the two men on the bridge in the Leeds pattern are taller. Swansea also produced a version with an insect border (11).

The Spode factory produced a considerable number of 'Chinese' patterns including one (13) on porcelain which is similar in many respects to the Swansea and Leeds examples. Williams calls this *The Temple* or *Willow Pattern* (p147). A Chinese prototype is referred to by J. K. des Fontaines (plate 134b) as *The Broseley Pattern*. In order to try to bring some order into the nomenclature, the descriptions used here pick out important distinguishing features in picture and border. The plates illustrated on page 17 are referred to as the Swansea and Leeds *Two-man/scroll Patterns* (10 and 12) and the Swansea and Spode *Two-man/insect Patterns* (11 and 13).

It would be quite impossible to describe all the early chinoiserie patterns produced in the eighteenth century and the first decade of the nineteenth century. Within ten years of Thomas Turner's first willow pattern, the underglaze techniques were being used by John Turner of Lane End who secured the services of William Underwood from Worcester; Josiah Spode of Stoke who employed Thomas Lucas and James Richards from Caughley; John Yates of Shelton who employed John Ainsworth from Caughley; and Joshua Heath of Hanley.

Between 1790 and 1800 other firms entered the field. These included the Castleford Pottery of David Dunderdale & Co in Yorkshire; John Davenport of Longport, Staffordshire; the Don Pottery at

10 (*above left*) *Cambrian Pottery, Swansea*
Two-man/scroll Pattern (A)
(*Courtesy: Hampshire County Museum Service. No 51 in Bignell Collection Catalogue, 1943*)
Indented plate (c1800) with chinoiserie pattern in dark-medium blue. Two pagodas are linked by a three-arch bridge on which there are two small figures. Other figures appear in the pagoda doorway and nearby. The picture is framed in a band with a cellular motif broken in four places by stylised flowers. The border is of geometrical motifs, flowers and Chinese writing scrolls.
Impressed mark: SWANSEA.
Diam 9.6in. Single foot rim. Pale greenish-blue rippled glaze.

11 (*above right*) *Cambrian Pottery, Swansea*
Two-man/insect Pattern (A)
Indented plate (c1800) with chinoiserie pattern in dark-medium blue very similar to (10) in all respects except for the border which has geometrical motifs, flowers and insects. The edge of the rim is painted over the glaze with an ochre colour.
Impressed mark: SWANSEA.
Diam 9.6in. Single foot rim. Pale greenish-blue rippled glaze.

12 (*below left*) *Leeds Pottery*
Two-man/scroll Pattern (A)
Indented plate (c1800) with chinoiserie pattern in dark blue, similar in nearly all respects to the Cambrian Pottery plate above (10) except that the figures are larger.
Impressed mark: LEEDS POTTERY.
Diam 9.7in. Single foot rim. Blue rippled glaze.

13 (*below right*) *Spode*
Two-man/insect Willow Pattern (A)
Saucer dish (c1790–1805), in medium blue, with a pagoda on the left and a single-arch bridge with two men facing the pagoda on the right. Other figures stand in the entrance to the pagoda and nearby. There is a straight fence in the foreground near a prominent willow tree, and a fence leads from the bridge towards the pagoda. The border has geometrical, scroll and insect motifs. The edge of the rim is gilded over the glaze.
Printed mark: SPODE.
Diam 8.3in. Prominent foot rim (0.3in). Clear glaze on porcelain body.

Swinton, Yorkshire; the Herculaneum and the Islington Potteries in Liverpool; possibly the Leeds Pottery which had its own engravers and printers for overglaze black-printed wares; Thomas Minton of Stoke who unfortunately did not mark his wares at this period; and the Cambrian Pottery in Swansea which had secured the services in 1790 of an engraver from Staffordshire, Thomas Rothwell (1742–1807).

The Herculaneum Pottery took this name when it was sold by Richard Abbey to Worthington, Humble & Holland in 1796, and it is assumed that wares printed in underglaze blue were made from this date. Occasionally the wares bear an actual date. The dish (14) decorated with chinoiserie bears an impressed mark for 1807. The pattern is identical with a Spode design (Williams, fig 104). It may be regarded as transitional between the dark-blue wares of the eighteenth century and the medium-blue wares of the 1810–30 period made for the British home market in which stipple engraving is combined with line engraving. The dish is printed in dark-medium blue and the shaded area around the pagoda is in a uniform coarse stipple. The stipple technique was not at this period used to produce fine gradations of tone.

It is usually possible to assign marked Herculaneum pieces to periods even when no date appears. The single word HERCULANEUM appears on wares before 1822. By this date the managers had decided to impress the full name HERCULANEUM POTTERY. When Thomas Case and John Mort took over the works in 1833 they introduced marks which included the Liver bird (GM 2011–12) and produced wares printed with views of Liverpool. A number of Herculaneum patterns are illustrated by Little (plates 107–12) and in Alan Smith's *Illustrated Guide to Liverpool Herculaneum Pottery* (1970).

The Spode dish (15) has a chinoiserie design usually referred to as *The 'Trophies-Nankin' Pattern*. It is line engraved with a vase, scrolls, and writing equipment, symbols of Chinese culture. A second version of this pattern was produced later (Williams, fig 122) in which stylised flowers decorate the 'antiques' and there is a border with pear-shaped medallions of flowers. This is *The 'Trophies-Etruscan' Pattern*. A third version is *The 'Trophies-Dagger' Pattern* (Whiter, plate 30) still made under the name of 'Fitzhugh'.

14 (above) Herculaneum

Two-man/two-arch pattern (A) *Indented dish (1807) with chinoiserie in dark-medium blue. The main features are a pagoda (right) and a two-arch bridge (left) on which two figures with arms raised face one another apparently in greeting. There is no willow tree. The foreground shows a masted boat flying a pennant. In the distance there are four boats with sails set, and ten birds in the sky forming a V. The shaded areas of land are of stipple engraving which can be seen clearly without magnification. The picture is framed within a band of 'Catherine-wheel scrolls'. The border design is geometrical and includes sprigs of flowers.*
Impressed mark: HERCULANEUM.
1807
Length 12.6in. Width 8.7in. No foot rim. Three single stilt marks on printed border and also on underside of rim. Very pale greenish-blue rippled glaze on white body.

15 (below) Spode

'Trophies-Nankin'
Earliest of 'Trophies' patterns
Small dish (c1795–1805) with chinoiserie pattern in three parts:
(a) The central area with stylised leaves and geometrical motifs, the whole bounded by a dagger border.
(b) The surrounding area with a pattern of vases, writing scrolls and ribbons which gives the name —'hundred antiques'.
(c) The border of geometrical motifs usually associated with willow-type patterns.
Impressed mark: Spode (in lower case letters).
Printed mark: Spode (in lower case letters).
Length 10.1in. Width 7in. No foot rim. Three single stilt marks on base. Rippled glaze with the faintest tinge of blue on white body.

EXPANSION AND DECLINE

The Adams Family

There were many potters in the Adams family and they have operated many potteries since the eighteenth century. The most notable for blue-printed ware were the Greengates Pottery, Tunstall, run by William Adams from c1769 to 1800 and then by his son Benjamin; and the Cliff Bank Works, Stoke-on-Trent, operated also by a William Adams and later by his sons. Most pieces marked with the name Adams were probably made at Stoke.

The wares which are printed in dark blue are now probably commoner in America than in Britain for there was a large export trade. Two series had a notable success: 'Columbus Views' which consisted of eight scenes showing the landing of Columbus and landscapes with Indians, and 'American Views' with fourteen subjects including the Falls of Niagara. One pattern shows Mitchell & Freeman's china and glass warehouse in Chatham Street, Boston (Moore, fig 60). 'English Views' included a series of scenes based on Regent's Park, London. The plate (16) shows a typical dark-blue *View of Whitby*. *The Native Pattern* (17) which is printed in a lighter blue has also been noted on later wares by F. & R. Pratt & Co Ltd of Fenton.

Samuel Alcock of Burslem

The plate (18) made by Samuel Alcock at Hill Pottery, Burslem, is a late example of blue-printed ware made c1830–5. It has interest because it was made for the Orange Society founded in Northern Ireland in 1794. In 1826 political societies were banned in Ireland but they were revived in 1828, when HRH the Duke of Cumberland was appointed Grand Master. There were then 175,000 members in Ireland and 140,000 in England, Wales and Scotland. By 1835 the movement was well established in the army and a parliamentary investigation led to the dissolution of the Orange Society in 1836, though it was later revived. William III was always honoured by the Orangemen as the man who rescued England from popery when he defeated James in the Battle of the Boyne in 1690.

Thomas & John Carey

It is very difficult to trace the history of this firm. It seems to have changed its name several times and to have operated more than one pottery,

16 (*above left*) *William Adams* 'View of Whitby' (*Courtesy: Hampshire County Museum Service. No 240 in the Bignell Collection Catalogue, 1943*) *Plate* (c1810–20), *in very dark blue, with a view of Whitby showing the harbour and a shipbuilding yard with a church tower on the hill behind. There are sailing ships and figures in the foreground. The scene is framed in a border of flowers, leaves and fruit which extends to the well of the plate. Impressed mark: ADAMS. STAFFORDSHIRE. WARRANTED around an impressed eagle (GM 19). Diam 9.4in. Double foot rim. Blue glaze.*

17 (*above right*) *William Adams* 'Native' *Pattern Indented plate* (c1820), *in medium blue, with a country scene showing cottages, a river spanned by a bridge with three arches, and mountains in the distance. Two equestrian ladies have dismounted and appear to be bargaining with a fisherman who kneels before them with his catch. The border of flowers against a dark cross-hatched background includes the leaves and flowers of convolvulus. Impressed mark: ADAMS (GM 18). Diam 10in. Single foot rim. Heavy greenish-blue rippled glaze.*

18 (*below left*) *Samuel Alcock* 'Japanese Design' with William III *Indented plate* (c1830–5), *in light blue, with the equestrian figure of William III surmounted by a ribbon with the words 'The Glorious & Immortal Memory'. The border extends to the well of the plate and has an outer stippled area with rococo scrolls; the inner area is of flowering thorn branches with exotic birds. Printed mark: 'Japanese' (in a cartouche of flowering thorn similar to border) surmounted by the word 'stoneware' and below S A & Co. Diam 10.4in. Rounded foot rim. Clear, slightly rippled glaze on white body with small black specks.*

19 (*below right*) *Thomas & John Carey* 'Lady of the Lake' *Pattern Indented plate* (c1825), *in medium blue, with pattern and mark as for 20. Diam 10in. Deeply dished rim. Narrow double foot rim. Blue rippled glaze on light white body weighing less than 14oz.*

though 'CAREYS' would appear to refer to Thomas & John Carey.

The sequence appears to have been as follows:

1818 Carey & Son of Lane End
1823 Thomas & John Carey of Lane End
1829 Thomas Carey of Lane Delph
1842 Thomas & John Carey of Lane End and Middle Fenton; partnership dissolved
1847 Thomas Carey died

The Carey pieces illustrated (19 and 20) are of very high quality. They are superbly engraved with an interesting composite pattern based on Sir Walter Scott's poem published in 1810. On the left is the *Lady of the Lake* on Loch Katrine in her 'little skiff'; on the right she sits 'upon a rock with lichens wild' while 'the harper on the islet beach' reclines 'against a blighted tree'. The fruit basket has been treated on handles and sides with a dark blue translucent glaze similar to that on some pieces by Rogers & Son.

Careys also produced a series of 'Cathedrals', including *Durham Cathedral* and *St Paul's Cathedral*. Margaret Macdonald's *Dictionary of Marks* (1962), p194, shows the mark used for this series printed on a body described as 'Carey's Saxon Stone China'. G. Woolliscroft Rhead in *British Pottery Marks* (1910) mentions a Carey pattern called *The Cottar's Saturday Night*. S. Laidaker (Part II, p20) describes a Careys series which was exported to America, with pictures of the Seats of Noblemen including Belvoir Castle; Castle Creke, Cork, Ireland; Eaton Hall; Shugborough Hall; Sutton Hoo and Woburn Abbey.

James & Ralph Clewes

These potters operated a pottery at Cobridge from 1817 to 1834 and produced large quantities of fine blue-printed earthenware, much of it for export to America. When the firm closed down in 1834 James Clews went to America and started a pottery at Troy, Indiana, but failed after two years because of lack of skilled labour and suitable raw materials. He then returned to England.

Clews' wares are normally of high quality and are much sought after, particularly the series with American views. The dish illustrated (21) as well as the jug (23) were produced for the English market. Both patterns have a background of fine-mesh net. It seems possible that the dish which has a pattern called *Coronation* may have been made either to commemorate the Coronation of George IV in 1821 or the accession of William IV in 1830.

20 (*above*) *Thomas & John Carey*
'The Lady of the Lake' Pattern
Fruit basket and stand (c1825) with the Lady of the Lake Pattern in dark-medium blue. To the left is the 'Lady of the Lake' in her skiff; to the right she is seated with the musician who holds a harp. The pierced border of the stand, the outside of the basket, and the two handles of the basket have all been treated with a translucent blue glaze, contrasting strongly with the clear glaze over the printed pattern and the inside of the basket.
Printed mark on basket and stand: Prince of Wales feathers surmounted by the title—LADY OF THE LAKE, with the maker's name CAREYS on a ribbon beneath.
Length of stand 11.0in. Height of basket with stand 3.3in.

21 (*below*) *James & Ralph Clews*
'Coronation' Pattern
(Courtesy: Hampshire County Museum Service. No 37 in Bignell Collection Catalogue, 1943)
Eight-sided dish (c1830) in medium blue with a pattern depicting a vase with flowers, fruit (peaches and pears) and a small bird (finch) on a marble table.
Impressed mark: STAFFORDSHIRE.CLEWS. WARRANTED between concentric circles which enclose a crown (GM 919).
Printed mark: CLEWS with an oval cartouche formed by a circular strap with buckle, bearing the pattern title—CORONATION. The cartouche is surmounted by a crown, and a thistle and rose are printed to left and right respectively.
Length 19in. Width 14½in. No foot rim. Pale blue rippled glaze.

It has not been possible to identify the river scene on the oval dish (22). No other pieces with this unusual border have so far been noted. The Clews brothers favoured series rather than individual patterns. These included:

(i) The *Select Scenery* series with topographical scenes which included abbeys and castles, etc (see Little, plate 18, and GI, plate 155). Some of these views may have been based on engravings in the six volumes of John Preston Neale's *Seats of Noblemen in England, Wales and Scotland* (1822).

(ii) *Zoological Garden Views* which include cages with birds and bears.

(iii) *Wilkie Pictures* based on paintings by David Wilkie. These include *The Valentine, The Escape of the Mouse, Christmas Eve, Playing at Draughts, Letter of Introduction, The Errant Boy* and the *Rabbit on the Wall.*

(iv) The *Doctor Syntax* series which contains at least 27 scenes based on Thomas Rowlandson's illustrations for William Combe's *Three Tours of Doctor Syntax* (1815–21) (see Little, plates 19 and 20).

(v) The *Don Quixote* series with over 20 scenes based on engravings from an illustrated edition of *The Adventures of Don Quixote de la Mancha.*

(vi) The *Aesop's Fables* series was based on drawings in *The Ladies Amusement* and a few on Barlow's original drawings. Forty-two examples have been recorded.

Clews used patterns from Spode's *Indian Sporting series* (p72) on export wares for America.

The most popular of the Clews patterns in America is *The Landing of the Lafayette* (1824) (see GI, plate 156).

Coalport Porcelain Works, Shropshire

The Coalport factory was established by John Rose in 1796. In 1799 he and his partners took over the nearby Caughley works where they continued to make porcelain transfer-printed in underglaze blue. The jug (24) was made between 1810 and 1815 before the Caughley pottery was demolished. Unglazed wasters with this pattern have been found on the site and G. A. Godden describes a teapot with the same printed Chinese-style seal mark linked with a printed mark 'C.B. Dale', or Coalbrookdale, a name often used to describe the wares of the firm (see the *Antique Dealer* and *Collector's Guide* [February 1968] fig VII, p46).

22 (*above*) *James & Ralph Clews*
River Scene with Fort (A)
Dish (1818–34), in medium blue, with a river scene. The bridge appears to be half-built, and the buildings on the bank of the river include a fort tower with armed soldiers on the battlements and a domed tower with wind vane. There is an angler on the river bank and two men who appear to have brought two large pitchers by boat, talking with two women. The border consists of flowers and leaves against a dark background.
Printed mark: CLEWS *across a pseudo-Chinese seal mark. Beneath are the words* 'Stone China'.
Length 14.9in. Width 11.6in. No foot rim. Blue rippled glaze unevenly applied. Much chipping of the glaze round the rim gives a delft-like appearance to the edge of the dish.

23 (*below left*) *James & Ralph Clews*
Basket and Vase Floral Pattern (A)
Jug (c1830), in dark-medium blue, with a pattern showing a basket and vases of flowers resting on a surface which carries shells and a box, the whole against a fine-mesh net background. The border around the top of the jug shows a stylised rose, scrolls and medallions, including a two-handled urn with flowers. The same motif is applied to the handle.
Printed mark with the word WARRANTED *across a pseudo-Chinese seal. Above is the maker's name* CLEWS. *Below are the words* IRONSTONE CHINA *on a ribbon.*
Height from base to rim 7.2in. Flattened base rim. Very blue rippled glaze.

24 (*below right*) *Coalport*
Two-man/insect Willow (or 'Broseley') *Pattern* (A)
Cream jug (c1810–15), in light blue, with a willow pattern showing two men on a single-arch bridge facing a large pagoda. Four 'apple' trees appear on this pattern with some 'windfalls' in other places. The border pattern is of geometrical motifs and insects.
Printed mark: a square pseudo-Chinese seal.
Height to top of handle 4in. Flattened foot rim with little glaze. Cream-coloured porcelain body showing distinctly brown to the light.

Cornfoot, Colville & Co

This firm operated the Low Lights Pottery at North Shields, Northumberland, from about 1829 until 1834 when it became Cornfoot, Patten & Co, and later Carr & Patten. By about 1850 it had changed its name once more to John Carr & Co, and by 1854 to J. Carr & Son. Although the engraving and transfer work on the illustrated example (25) has been quite well done, the quality of the body and glaze is below standard for the period.

A number of other Newcastle potteries produced blue and white transfer ware early in the nineteenth century including Forth Bank Pottery (Wallace & Co from 1838); Ouseburn Pottery (Robert Maling from 1817); St Anthony's Pottery (Sewell & Donkin from 1828); St Peter's Pottery (Thomas Fell from 1817); the Sheriff Hill Pottery (Patterson & Co from c1830) and Stepney Bank Pottery (Davies, Cookson & Wilson from 1822) which used the *Country Church Pattern*.

John Davenport

When John Davenport started to make blue-printed wares soon after he had established his pottery at Longport c1795, he was already an experienced potter. His earlier blue-printed wares are of high quality but there was some deterioration after about 1830 and, as the firm continued to produce earthenwares until 1887, it is important for the collector to attempt to date pieces. Fortunately, this is not too difficult. Most Davenport wares were marked, though it is important to remember that when dinner services were made up of as many as 120 pieces some makers decided to mark only a limited number of the pieces. Early Davenport wares often carry a small impressed anchor (26) or the maker's name 'Davenport' in lower case letters, or both. An anchor with 'DAVENPORT' in upper case letters was used after 1805. There may be some overlap in the use of these early marks but in general they may be regarded as having been used before about 1820. Subsequently many pieces carried a printed mark, often with the pattern name.

In 1830 John Davenport retired and his sons, William and Henry, took over. By 1835, possibly earlier, the firm started to include year numbers in the mark. These were placed on either side of the anchor. Godden illustrates part of a dinner service with '3' and '5' indicating a date of 1835 (GI, colour plate V). This shows the introduction of other colours in addition to blue. A plate in the author's collection, dated 1836, is printed in green and there

25 (above left) Cornfoot, Colville & Co
Country Church Pattern (A)
Slightly indented plate (c1829–34), in medium blue, with a country scene of a church with spire, and cottages. Two anglers fish in a pond; a man and woman stand talking on either side of a four-barred gate. The border is bounded on either side by stringing and is of two types of flower placed alternately against a stippled background: the leaves in a darker blue.
Impressed mark: CORNFOOT COLVILLE & CO forming a circle.
Diam 9.2in. Rounded foot rim. Greenish-blue rippled glaze.
(This specimen was acquired by the Laing Art Gallery and Museum, Newcastle-upon-Tyne in 1970.)

26 (above right) John Davenport
Chinoiserie Ruins Pattern (A)
Indented plate (c1800), in medium blue, with a chinoiserie pattern with tropical trees and a ruin. The view includes two fences, and a standing figure with sunshade talking to a seated figure. The border repeats the tropical trees motif.
Impressed mark: a small anchor.
Diam 7.9in. No foot rim. Very pale blue strongly rippled glaze on white body.

27 (below) John Davenport
Chinoiserie Bridgeless Pattern (A)
Indented and pierced basket stand (c1810), in medium blue, with chinoiserie pattern. On either side of a stretch of water are pagodas, on the right with a man in the doorway, on the left with an outsize fence. A man is propelling a boat by using a pole. The picture is framed by an unprinted pierced band. The border has geometrical and insect motifs.
Impressed mark: Davenport (in lower case letters) curving above an anchor (GM 1181).
Length 10.1in. Width 7.9in. Rounded foot rim. Pale green rippled glaze on creamware body.

is a printed cartouche which describes the pattern as *Scott's Illustrations: Waverley*. Another printed mark on this plate gives the name of the American agents, HENDERSON & GAINES, IMPORTERS, 45 CANAL ST., NEW ORLEANS.

The Chinoiserie Ruins Pattern (26) seems to have been a best seller. A large number of pieces have been noted in various parts of the country. Godden gives the production date as c1795–1805 (GI, p117). An unmarked piece with this pattern has been noted with a foot rim (unlike the marked Davenport pieces). This pattern was also used by Job Ridgway (c1802–8). See G. A. Godden's *Ridgway Porcelains* 1972, plate 1. Most Davenport pieces of this period are of excellent quality and are well glazed. This is not surprising since John Davenport was also a glassmaker.

The Chinoiserie Bridgeless Pattern (27) is not uncommon. This particular example, however, is unusual in that it is printed on creamware and the glaze shows distinctly green where it has run against the foot rim. Davenport basket stands *do* have foot rims.

Three other chinoiserie patterns, two early (28 and 30) and one a little later (29), confirm the view that such designs were an important part of the output. However, other patterns were introduced at a very early stage, certainly before 1810 and perhaps earlier. One of the earliest must have been *The Tudor Mansion Pattern* (31). This plate, except for the actual pattern, is similar in every way to the plate with *The Chinoiserie Ruins Pattern* (26). It has the same type of engraving, body and glaze, and it bears the name 'Davenport' in lower case letters.

It would perhaps be useful at this stage to emphasise once again the danger of accepting the statements made by earlier writers which have been repeated *ad nauseam* in later publications. It has recently been stated that John Davenport potted willow pattern services 'by the ton'. What proof have we of this statement? In nine years of searching the author has only noted a single unmarked willow pattern plate which could be reasonably attributed to Davenport, yet other Davenport pieces are by no means uncommon. Surely, if there had been such a large output, pieces would turn up more frequently? Or has some earlier writer wrongly called *The Chinoiserie Bridgeless Pattern* a willow pattern? Every clue one follows in the study of blue and white transfer ware leads to the conclusion that patterns have nearly always been inadequately described. It is for this reason that

28 (above) *John Davenport*
View of the Imperial Park at Gehol Dish (c1810–15), *printed in dark-medium blue, with a chinoiserie design showing a boat with sail ferrying passengers across a river. A mandarin-figure with servant waits on the bank. A number of buildings are seen including a tall pagoda on the hill. A luxuriant willow-type tree hangs across the river. The border has geometrical and dragon motifs but the English floral border against a stippled ground has pushed it towards the edge of the dish.*
Impressed mark: Davenport (in lower case letters) curving above an anchor (GM 1181).
Length 14.5in. Width 11.2in. No foot rim. Clear rippled glaze on white body.
(*Note:* This scene is now known to have been taken from John Barrow's *Travels in China* published by T. Cadell & W. Davies in 1806.)

29 (below) *John Davenport*
Bamboo and Peony Pattern (A)
Eight-sided indented dish (c1815–25), printed in dark-medium blue, with a bamboo and peony pattern which includes a fence. The design is framed by a band of 'Catherine-wheel scrolls'. The border, which has geometrical motifs with stylised flowers, is restricted to the rim.
Impressed mark: DAVENPORT (in capitals) curving above an anchor.
Length 14.5in. Width 12.6in. No foot rim. Clear rippled glaze.

full details have been given in the captions to the illustrations in this book including information about size, glaze and body.

By about 1810 John Davenport appears to have introduced a number of patterns with the type of floral border that became so popular in Regency days. The three examples illustrated (32, 33 and 34) were almost certainly made before John Davenport's retirement in 1830. *The Mare and Foal Pattern* appears to have been one of a series of country scenes which all carried the same border. There is an example with a different scene but with the same border in the pottery collection of the Hampshire County Museum Service.

The whole subject of borders is a fascinating one. These are some quotations from books published in the last twenty years:

'Find the border and you have the maker and the rest is easy.' (1954)

'The makers of some unmarked specimens have been identified by their border patterns, which were not pirated by competing potters as were successful designs for the main pictorial ornament.' (1961)

'It was unusual before 1830 for the same border design to be used by more than one potter.' (1969)

It would be very convenient if these statements were accurate. The third one is wisely cautious but evidence accumulates to show that it was by no means as unusual as has previously been supposed for two potters to use the same border. Individual potters used a great variety of borders though perhaps selecting one border pattern for a series with a common theme. It will be seen that the ten Davenport pieces illustrated (26–35) all carry different border patterns. Little illustrates two other patterns (plates 23 and 24) which again have different borders. So a border was certainly not regarded as the 'trade-mark' of a potter for all his wares. Most potters seemed to feel that a new pattern demanded a new border to go with it, and a new series of patterns a special 'series border'.

It must be remembered that among the many firms operating in Staffordshire there were some that failed and had to sell their stock. This sometimes included copper plates which could then be used by another potter. When the stock of the Turner factory was finally sold in 1823 the auctioneers advertised an 'Excellent Stock of Earthenware, Potters' Utensils, Copper plate engravings, etc', and among the lots were, for example, '1 tea set, temple pattern complete in 8 plates' and a 'table service of

30 (top left) John Davenport
Chinoiserie High Bridge Pattern (A) *Dished indented plate (c1810–15), in medium blue, with a pagoda on a rock by the riverside. A pathway which crosses the river by a high bridge leads to a second pagoda on a more distant hill. There are three figures on a patio by the river bank, one seated, one standing and smoking a long-stemmed pipe, the third apparently trying to attract some men in a boat. The border has flowers and fruit (pears) and a waterfall tumbling over rocks (left). Impressed mark: Davenport (in lower case letters). Diam 9.8in. Single foot rim. Fine blue rippled glaze.*

31 (top right) John Davenport
Tudor Mansion Pattern (Oxburgh Hall) (A) *Indented plate (c1810–15), in medium blue, with a country scene showing a Tudor mansion between tall trees. Two figures, a standing man and a seated boy, hold what would appear to be a net and a rod respectively. The border is made of branches from the type of trees seen in the picture. Impressed mark: Davenport (in lower case letters) above a small anchor (GM 1181). Diam 8.1in. No foot rim. Clear rippled glaze.*

32 (below left) John Davenport
Mosque and Fishermen Pattern (A) *Indented plate (c1815–30), in medium blue, with an imaginary scene showing a mosque in an English landscape and a river with three negro fishermen in a covered boat. The border which descends to the well of the plate is mainly of wild roses against a stippled ground which is darker and cross-hatched near the edge of the plate. Impressed mark: DAVENPORT (in capitals) curved above an anchor. Diam 9.6in. Single foot rim. Clear rippled glaze.*

33 (below right) John Davenport
The Villagers Pattern (A) *Slightly indented plate (c1815–30), in medium blue. A village scene with a church tower. A boy is blowing bubbles from a pipe watched by a standing woman and a sprawling child while a dog looks on. The shading in the foreground is cross-hatched line engraving. The border is of flowers and scrolls against a stipple ground. Impressed mark: DAVENPORT curved above an anchor. Diam 9.8in. Single foot rim. Rippled blue glaze.*

11 plates, spring pattern, with block and working mould to match, (Hillier, p75).

The Davenport mug (35) is the only example illustrated with the maker's name 'DAVENPORT' printed in underglaze blue. Printed marks seldom appear on the wares until about 1820 and most of them are a good deal later. This particular mug probably dates from about 1830 and appears to have been used as a scoop, for one side of the rim is badly worn away. A printed mark on another piece describes the design as *Muleteer*. A dinner service of 105 pieces with this pattern sold for £64 in 1964.

It is not known to what extent John Davenport competed in the export market. He certainly sent wares to America but there is no record of special American designs. Some wares were sold to New Orleans dealers called Hill & Henderson, probably the firm that became Henderson & Gaines in the 1830s (see p28), but whether blue-printed services were included is not known.

Some export wares went to India. A special dinner service was made for the Madras Artillery showing the Seringapatam Medal as a centre-piece surrounded by the battle honours. The border used for this service was identical to that with *The Bamboo and Peony Pattern* (29).

Don Pottery

The Don Pottery at Swinton in Yorkshire, like the Davenport factory, was in existence for a long period—from 1790 to 1893—but it is fairly easy to distinguish the early wares made before the pottery was sold to Samuel Barker in 1834, provided they are marked, though many pieces were left unmarked. The commonest mark, impressed or printed, is DON or DON POTTERY with or without the name of the proprietor GREEN. After c1820 the crest mark of a lion holding a flag was used (GM 1314).

It seems probable that blue-printed wares were made at Swinton in the 1790s; chinoiserie patterns were certainly produced. But the most interesting designs were the 'Named Italian Views'.

The series which was produced between 1810 and 1834 included:

Tomb of Theron at Aggrigentum; Ruins near Aggrigenti; View of Alicata; Ruins of the Castle at Canna; Obelisque at Catania; Ancient Cistern at Catania; View of Ceragliano; Monastery at Fra Castagne; Cascade at Isola; View of Palma; Grotto

34 (*above left*) *John Davenport*
The Mare and Foal Pattern (A)
Slightly indented plate (c1815–30), in medium blue, with a riverside country scene with mare and foal. The border of scrolls and flowers which descends to the well of the plate is partially against a stippled background which is restricted to the rim.
Impressed mark: DAVENPORT (*in capitals*) *curved above an anchor.*
Diam 8.2in. Single foot rim. Clear colourless glaze.

35 (*above right*) *William Davenport & Co*
'The Muleteer' Pattern
Mug (c1835–40), printed in medium blue, with a river scene with gothic church, waterfall, castle on a hill and in the foreground a man mounted on a mule. The border inside the mug is composed of flowers and C-scrolls against a stipple ground. The handle carries a spray of flowers.
Printed mark: DAVENPORT.
Height 3.3in. Single foot rim. Smooth colourless glaze.

36 (*below*) *Don Pottery*
'Named Italian Views' Series:
'Residence of Solimenes, near Vesuvius'
Strainer (c1820–34), in medium blue, with a scene showing the residence of Solimenes among trees with groups of figures in the foreground and a mounted horseman leading a prancing white horse. The title of the scene is printed below the picture.
Impressed mark: DON POTTERY, *also B, CVX and 16 scattered near the maker's mark.*
Printed mark: Crest mark of a lion erased carrying a banner, and the words DON POTTERY (*GM 1314*).
Length 12.5in. Width 9.3in. Smooth blue glaze.

of St Rosalie near Palermo; Temple of Serapis at Pouzguoli; Residence of Solimenes near Vesuvius; View of Taormina; Terrace of the Naval Amphitheatre at Taorminum; View of the Valley of Oretho near Palermo.

The Foley Pottery, Fenton

The name 'Elkin' or 'Elkins' occurs in the title of a number of Staffordshire pottery firms after 1822. The first appears to be Elkins & Co of Lane End which operated from 1822 to 1830 and produced a series of views of historic houses under the title *Irish Scenery*. The same border was used for the whole series. An example is illustrated (38) and Little shows another scene (plate 25). In 1822 a partner called Knight appears to have joined the firm and a pottery was established at Foley, Fenton. It seems to have started as Elkin, Knight & Co, and in 1827 to have become Elkin, Knight & Bridgwood, though it was sometimes called Knight, Elkin & Co, or Knight, Elkin & Bridgwood. The forms which start with 'Knight' appear to be later. Perhaps Mr Elkin died and was succeeded by his son; if so, the older partner, Mr Knight, might well have then wished that his name should come first. However, the products of the Foley Pottery are not difficult to recognise. The designs are engraved so that they stand out in white against a stippled ground printed in light blue tinged with violet. A notable series, of which three patterns have so far been noted, is described in a scrolled cartouche as *Etruscan* with the maker's initials 'E.K.B.' These consist of classical scenes which are not easy to identify, nor is it possible to say where they originated. Other makers used similar designs: Joseph Clementson of Hanley used a pattern in 1849 called *Nestor's Sacrifice* (see GI, plate 154) which was derived directly from one of Flaxman's designs for Homer's *Odyssey*, engraved by Thomas Piroli in Rome in 1793. The jug (41) with the *Moss Rose* pattern bears the initials 'K.E.B.' and is probably a later production when the firm had become Knight, Elkin & Bridgwood.

37 (above left) Don Pottery
'Named Italian Views' Series:
'A View in Palma'
Plate (c1810–30), in dark-medium blue, with a scene showing classical buildings and a column surmounted by a cross. A procession of monks carrying a coffin towards a church is followed by a monk of higher status who reads from a book, his train held by another monk. Below the picture are the words 'A View of Palma'. The border is mainly of flowers against a stipple ground with leaves, an urn and two putti carrying flowers.
Unmarked.
Diam 10in. No foot rim. Very blue glaze.

38 (above right) Elkins & Co
'Irish Scenery' Series
Plate (1822–30), in medium blue, with a scene showing a large country house, a river with sailing boat and a man in the foreground with a bundle on his back, driving a laden horse. The picture is framed by the key-pattern edge of the stippled ground of the border which consists of rococo scrolls and flowers.
Printed mark: The royal arms carrying an inescutcheon with a crown above and ribbons below bearing the motto 'Dieu et Mon Droit' and below that again IRISH SCENERY. ELKINS & CO.
Diam 10in. Double foot rim. Smooth slightly blue glaze unevenly applied.
(Note: Several English scenes were included under this series title.)

39 (below) Elkin, Knight & Bridgwood
'Etruscan' Series. Britannia Pattern (A)
Dish (1827–40), with wavy edge, decorated with moulded beading, printed in light blue (tinged with violet) with a classical pattern on a stippled background. It shows Britannia with shield and spear seated with three maidens and a child around her. Two small lion symbols appear on her person—one on her helmet and one on her breast. The inner band which frames the picture consists of a garland of leaves. The border pattern is of scrolls and acanthus leaves.
Printed mark: ETRUSCAN on a stippled ground within scrolls, the whole forming a cartouche. Below are the letters E.K.B.
Length 16.3in. Width 12.2in. No foot rim. Greyish blue, slightly rippled glaze unevenly applied.

Thomas Fell of Newcastle

Thomas Fell operated St Peter's Pottery, Newcastle, over a long period. The pottery was established in 1817 and the early wares made before 1830 bear the impressed mark 'FELL' or 'FELL NEWCASTLE'. After 1830 the name is followed by '& Co'. *The Tomb Pattern* (42) is a relatively early example of a tea bowl and saucer printed in dark blue. The design may have been produced in 1817 or, more likely in 1818, when the nation was mourning the death of Princess Charlotte. If so, it must be one of Fell's earliest patterns.

The Woodman Pattern (43) is a direct copy of a Spode pattern both in picture and border. According to L. Jewitt in *The Ceramic Art of Great Britain* (1883) the Spode factory introduced its *Woodman* pattern in 1816. Williams regards it as 'a composite picture taken from engravings of the period, the figure of the woman from a Kaufmann original and the landscape and man's figure either a Morland or of the Morland School' (p181). It is interesting to note that the Fell version is a mirror image of the Spode pattern. In the Spode pattern the woodman is on the right; in the Fell version on the left. It seems likely that an engraver working for Fell copied the pattern from a Spode transfer paper rather than from an example of the printed wares. In the Spode version (Williams, plates 136 and 137) the border and picture together cover the whole surface of a plate; in the Fell version there is an unprinted area between border and picture and the border transfer has been badly trimmed before application.

It should be noted that Thomas Godwin produced a completely different pattern with figures in a rural setting, some time after 1834, which was also called the *Woodman* pattern.

After 1830 Fell & Co continued to produce blue-printed wares but quality declined. An example of *The Wild Rose Pattern* (see p48) has been noted with the impressed anchor mark (GM 1532) together with a printed shield supported by two sea horses above a ribbon carrying the maker's name.

40 (*above left*) Elkin, Knight & Bridgwood
'Etruscan' Series
(*Courtesy: Mrs Elizabeth Carter*)
Dished plate (c1827–40), with wavy edge decorated with moulded beading, printed in light blue (tinged with violet) with a classical pattern on a stippled background. As in the dish in plate 39, the lion motif is prominent. The inner band which frames the picture is a garland of leaves. The border pattern is of scrolls and acanthus leaves.
Printed mark: ETRUSCAN on a stippled ground within scrolls, the whole forming a cartouche. Below the cartouche the letters E.K.B.
Diam 8.7in. No foot rim. Greyish blue slightly rippled glaze on white body.

41 (*above right*) Knight, Elkin & Bridgwood
'Moss-Rose' Pattern
Jug (c1834–40), in light blue, with moss roses on a stippled ground. The border of leaves and scrolls. A row of small flowers decorates the handle.
Printed mark: MOSS-ROSE No 35 within a cartouche beneath which is the maker's mark—K E & B.
Height from base to rim 5.5in. Single foot rim. Very pale bluish-green glaze.

42 (*below*) Thomas Fell   The Tomb Pattern (A)
Tea bowl and saucer (c1817–30), in dark blue with a picture showing a lady and child weeping at a tomb. The picture is framed by serpentine bands and there is a border of eight floral medallions against a line engraved ground.

FELL
Impressed mark on saucer only: NEWCASTLE *printed in a curve. Also the letter B.*
Diam of bowl 3.1in and of saucer 5.3in. Both have rims. Greenish-blue glaze.

Thomas & Benjamin Godwin

The New Wharf and New Basin potteries at Burslem were operated by Thomas & Benjamin Godwin between c1809 and 1834. The example illustrated (44) is of considerable interest because the title names a particular place on the Indus plain in India—Surseya Ghaut, Khanpore. However, it is not known whether it was made for export to India or not; it was probably taken from a drawing or engraving of the scene. After 1834 when Thomas Godwin continued the firm alone, he still decorated the borders of his blue-printed wares with scrolled medallions (GI, plate 275). The ability to use colours other than blue seems to have acted as a stimulus, for the firm began to build a thriving export trade to America and quality improved. One of the best known series includes six scenes in which William Penn is shown with the Indians when the 'William Penn Treaty' was signed (earlier writers have wrongly attributed this series to Thomas Green).

Ralph Hall of Tunstall

The pottery at Swan Bank, Tunstall, was operated by Ralph Hall from 1822 to c1836 and then became Ralph Hall & Son. In 1841 it became R. Hall & Co. Before 1822 Ralph Hall had been in partnership for some twenty years with John Hall and was therefore an experienced potter. The most interesting wares appear to have been produced in the 1820s. These have a very wide border of fruit and flowers and the picture, always of a named locality, occupies only a small part of the printed surface. Ralph Hall used a dark blue colour which was much in favour for American export wares at this period. The 'Select Views' series includes:

Biddulph Castle, Staffs (45)
Boughton Castle, Northants
Bramber Church, Sussex
Castle Prison, St Albans
Conway Castle, Carnarvon
Eashing Park, Surrey
Gryn, Flintshire
Luscombe, Devon
Pain's Hill, Surrey (46)
St Charles' Church
Valle Crucis Abbey
Warleigh House, Somerset
Wilderness, Kent

Another series entitled 'Picturesque Scenery', which has a border of large flowers, includes Broadlands, Hampshire; Dunsany Castle, Ireland; Fulham Church, Middlesex; Llanarth Court, Mon.

43 (top left) Thomas Fell   'Woodman' Pattern Plate (c1817–30), in medium blue, with a scene in which a woodman, standing with an axe in his right hand, is talking to a woman, seated on a tree trunk, holding a small child on her lap. There is a basket at her feet. In the background is a church spire.
Impressed mark: FELL (in large capitals).
Diam 8.8in. Single foot rim. Greenish-blue glaze unevenly applied.

43 (top left) Thomas & Benjamin Godwin
'Surseya Ghaut' Pattern Indented plate (c1825–34), in light blue, with a river scene on the Indus plain in India showing several boats and a flight of steps leading to a temple. The border which descends to the well of the plate has two pairs of Indian scenes each in a cartouche of scrolls, grapes and vine leaves. These alternate with larger bunches of grapes.
Printed mark: SURSEYA GHAUT
                    KHANPORE
                    T & B G
within a cartouche of scrolls and flowers.
Diam 10.4in. Single foot rim. Colourless glaze.

45 (bottom left) Ralph Hall 'Select Views' Series: 'Biddulph Castle, Staffs'
(Courtesy: Hampshire County Museum Service. No 237 in Bignell Collection Catalogue, 1943)
Indented dished plate (c1822–41), in a very dark blue, with a small picture of Biddulph Castle with a rider on a white horse, a dog and two standing figures in the foreground. The picture is framed in scrolls and the wide border of fruit and flowers extends to the well of the plate.
Printed mark:
    R. HALL'S SELECT VIEWS
    BIDDULPH CASTLE, STAFFORDSHIRE
    STONE CHINA all enclosed in a cartouche.
Diam 9.5in. Double foot rim. Rippled blue glaze.

46 (bottom right) Ralph Hall
            'Select Views' Series: 'Pains Hill, Surrey'
(Courtesy: Hampshire County Museum Service. No 239 in Bignell Collection Catalogue, 1943)
Indented dished plate (c1822–41), in a very dark blue, with a small picture of Pains Hill, Surrey, showing horse-riders in the parkland. The same border is used as in 45.
Printed mark: R. HALL'S SELECT VIEWS
                    PAINS HILL, SURREY
                    STONE CHINA
Diam 9.5in. Double foot rim. Rippled blue glaze.

Robert Hamilton of Stoke

Robert Hamilton learnt his trade as a potter from his father-in-law, Thomas Wolfe, who had already spent some fifteen years making blue-printed wares before they formed the partnership of Wolfe and Hamilton c1800. The partnership lasted until 1811 in which year Robert Hamilton started to operate a pottery in Stoke on his own. This continued until 1826.

In view of the opportunities for gaining experience, it is surprising to find that the wares he produced (47 and 48) lack quality. Although the actual transfer work has been well done, the printing has a blurred appearance suggesting either that worn plates were used or that the inking had been badly done. The thick glaze is gritty and is rough to the touch. Small bubbles have burst leaving 'craters' in the surface.

Several unmarked pieces have been noted with *The Fisherman with Nets Pattern* printed crisply in a lighter blue and well glazed. It is difficult to believe that these came from the same factory; perhaps another maker used the same pattern.

Charles Heathcote & Co of Lane End

The Heathcote pottery lasted for only six years, from 1818 to 1824, but during that time some fine blue-printed wares were made. The dish (49) is a typical example. This pattern seems to have been used on many domestic wares; examples have been noted on candle-holders as well as dinner services. Hillier (p76) mentions the fact that 'the Hanley Museum has a marked Heathcote plate and a marked Turner plate with identical underglaze printing'. He concludes that Heathcote bought some engraved plates from the Turner factory. Some copper plates were certainly sold when John Turner's personal effects were auctioned in 1815 but that was three years before Heathcote's business was established. The main stock of copper-plate engravings from the Turner factory was sold in 1829, five years after Heathcote ceased production. Moreover, Heathcote's work is crisp and clear and does not appear to have been transfer-printed from worn plates. Perhaps an engraver from the Turner factory joined the Heathcote firm and engraved afresh some of the patterns he had used in his previous employment. The fact that pieces with the same pattern can bear the imprint of more than one pottery emphasises once again the difficulty of attributing unmarked specimens.

47 (*above left*) *Robert Hamilton*
Ruined Castle Pattern (A)
Indented plate (1811–26), in dark blue, with a river scene including a ruined castle and three-arch bridge, distant figures and cows standing in the water. The picture is separated from the border by a narrow band of decoration. The border is of flowers against a stipple ground near the face of the plate and a darker line-engraved ground near the edge where there is a narrow bank of leaf decoration.
HAMILTON
Impressed mark: STOKE   (GM 1901)
Diam 9.8in. No foot rim. Pale blue glaze very poorly applied on the face of the plate which is covered with dark gritty spots.

48 (*above right*) *Robert Hamilton*
Fishermen with Nets Pattern (A)
Indented plate (1811–26), in dark blue, with a slightly blurred lakeside scene of fishermen hanging out their nets to dry on a tree. A building with Palladian pillared portico stands on the shore of the lake and there are mountains in the distance. The picture is separated from the border of flowers, grapes and vine leaves, by stringing.
HAMILTON
Impressed mark: STOKE
Diam 9.8in. No foot rim. Pale blue glaze which has contained bubbles which have burst on the face to leave 'moons'.

49 (*below*) *Charles Heathcote & Co*
Cattle and River Pattern (A)
Eight-sided dish (c1818–24), in medium blue, with a scene showing a country mansion in parkland sloping down to a lake or stream. Horses graze on the slopes, cows drink at the water. A man with stick and basket is resting at the water's edge. The border carries an elaborate scrolled design.
Impressed mark: HEATHCOTE & CO.
Length 16.4in. Breadth 12.4in. No foot rim. Rippled glaze.

The Standard Willow Pattern

A Herculaneum plate (50), though of rather poor quality, is of interest as an early example of *The Standard Willow Pattern*. The single impressed mark HERCULANEUM suggests a date prior to 1822 when the managers decided to add the word 'POTTERY' to their mark. Indeed, this plate could have been made much earlier. It is thought that the Spode factory may have introduced this *Standard Willow* design which has been used by hundreds of potters ever since. By 1830 it was certainly a very popular pattern, perhaps because it was said to tell the story of two lovers pursued by the girl's father over a bridge, a story popular with children. It is worth noting that in 1845, when *Punch* was hitting out at the low teaching standards in the new School of Design at Somerset House, a drawing was published headed 'The School of Bad Design' in which a student is seen copying the standard willow pattern from a large dish hanging on the wall. The caption reads: 'The study of "High Art" at Somerset House'.

Hicks, Meigh & Johnson of Shelton

The firm of Hicks & Meigh dates from 1806. It became Hicks, Meigh & Johnson in 1822, trading until 1835. Relatively few pieces bear the maker's name; most carry an early version of the royal arms (GM 2020 and 2022). Some of their stone china wares carry a double foot rim painted a buff colour underglaze; this is a feature that has not been noted on the wares of other potters.

The plate (52), with the arms of the Salters' Company, bears on the back the words *Du Croz, Skinner Street, London* above the usual mark. This is a plate from a large service purchased by the Salters' Company in 1827. When a new service was acquired at a later date, also from Du Croz, pieces from the old service were distributed among the members. Some earlier writers have assumed Du Croz to be a Staffordshire potter. *Robson's London Directory* described John Du Croz of 7 Skinner Street as an 'art glass and lamp manufacturer' who apparently also operated as a china dealer. From 1833 another glass manufacturing firm, Pike & Millidge, shared the premises with Du Croz. From 1836 to 1838 the Du Croz business was Du Croz & Co, and in 1838 Du Croz & Millidge. The directory describes the premises at this date as a 'china warehouse'. In 1842 John C. Du Croz is listed as a 'china and glass dealer' at 138 Regent Street, London.

50 (above left) Herculaneum
'Standard Willow Pattern'
Dished plate (c1820), deeply indented, printed in dark blue, with the standard willow pattern with pagoda, fence in foreground, three men on a three-arch bridge and two birds in the sky. The picture is framed in a band of geometrical design and the border is also composed of geometrical motifs with small flowers and scrolls.
Impressed mark: HERCULANEUM (in small capitals).
Diam 9.9in. Single foot rim. Very blue rippled glaze, 'gritty' in places.

51 (above right) Hicks & Meigh
Exotic Birds and Flowers Pattern (A)
Indented dished plate (c1820), printed in medium blue, with a pattern of exotic birds and flowers and with a flower-and-scroll border.
Printed mark: early version of the royal arms with the words STONE CHINA and No 9 beneath (GM 2020).
Diam 9.2in. Double foot rim painted underglaze in a buff colour. Single prominent stilt marks. Smooth colourless glaze. Body very heavy, weighing 19oz.

52 (below) Hicks, Meigh & Johnson
Salters' Company Dinner Service
Twelve-sided indented plate (1827) with moulded gadrooned edge, printed in medium blue with the arms of the Salters' Company framed in a ropework band with leaves of acanthus type. The border has stringing close to the gadrooned edge from which sprays of flowers extend towards the well of the plate.
Printed mark: The royal arms above the words Stone China in old English lettering and the figure 51 (GM 2022). Above this mark is printed DU CROZ, Skinner Street, London.
Diam 10.4in. Double foot rim painted underglaze in a buff colour. Prominent single stilt marks. Colourless glaze.

Jones & Son of Hanley

Very little is known about this potter. Godden gives the dates of operation as c1826–8 (GM, p364). All that is known is that a fine series was produced with the title 'British History' (53 and 54). The designs are attractive, well engraved and transferred, and they have an appropriate border. The following have been recorded:

Caractacus before Claudius; Alfred as a Minstrel; Signing of the Magna Carta (see *Trans English Ceramic Society*, 7, Part 2 [1969], plate 138c); Interview between Wallace and Bruce; Charles I ordering the Speaker to give up the Five Members; Hampden mortally wounded; Cromwell dismissing the Long Parliament; The Seven Bishops conveyed to the Tower; Landing of William of Orange; Death of General Wolfe; Death of Lord Nelson (53); Battle of Waterloo; Coronation of George IV; and Canute reproving his Courtiers.

It is possible that the firm continued as Elijah Jones of Hall Lane, Hanley, until 1831.

Leeds Pottery

It is not possible to date accurately the first blue-printed wares produced by Hartley, Greens & Co at Leeds but there seems to be no doubt that fine quality services with chinoiserie printed in a deep blue colour on pearlware and well-glazed were made by the first decade of the nineteenth century (see pp16–17). These early examples are line-engraved and show no sign of stipple work. Little (plate 96) illustrates a mug attributed to this period. The scene 'after Claude Lorraine' (55) is printed on creamware, though examples have also been noted on pearlware, and bears a LEEDS POTTERY mark. This pattern was also used by J. & R. Riley (Little, plate 52). It is not easy to decide which firm introduced the pattern or whether the second user pirated it, purchased plates, or was supplied with the plates by an outside engraver. Little illustrates another pattern used by the Leeds Pottery with men and horses in a romantic landscape (plate 98). The border bears a single passionflower. Eight Leeds patterns are listed by D. Towner in *The Leeds Pottery* (1963), pp42–4.

The Mason Family

After several years in partnership with Thomas Wolfe and John Lucock at the Islington Pottery, Liverpool, Miles Mason returned to his home

53 (*above left*) *Jones & Son*
'British History' Series: 'Death of Lord Nelson' (*Courtesy: Morris Tucker*)
Fruit dish (c1826–8), in medium blue, with a scene showing the death of Lord Nelson. This decorates the bowl of the dish which carries a border with alternate motifs showing respectively the crown and mitre, and a group of military and naval accoutrements. The sides of the dish show other scenes from the British History Series and the base repeats the border pattern.
Printed mark (see 54): Britannia and the seated figure of a woman to right and left of a gothic archway surmounted by a crown. Below the crown are the words BRITISH HISTORY. Within the archway the title of the pattern DEATH OF LORD NELSON. On a tablet beneath the archway the maker's name JONES & SON.
The dish is 11.3in by 9.1in, and the height from base to rim 4.1in.

54 (*above right*) *Jones & Son*
'British History' series: 'Death of Lord Nelson'.
Part of the base of the fruit dish (53) to show printed mark in underglaze blue.

55 (*below left*) *Leeds Pottery*
'Scene after Claude Lorraine'
Dished plate (c1810–20), in light blue, with a scene showing a classical building on a rocky promontory above a river which is crossed by a bridge of which two arches are visible. There are boatmen on the river and two goats with a man on the river bank. The border is made up of trees with a bridge, a Tudor gothic gateway, and domestic buildings.
Impressed mark: LEEDS POTTERY (*in small capitals*).
Diam 8.2in. No foot rim. Almost colourless rippled glaze on creamware body.

56 (*below right*) *Miles Mason*
Chinoiserie Pattern (A)
Saucer dish (c1810–16), light-medium blue, with chinoiserie including two pagoda-like structures, trees and figures. The border with geometrical designs including a cellular motif and scrolls.
Printed pseudo-Chinese seal mark (GM 2545).
Diam 8.4in. Single foot rim. Smooth colourless glaze on bone china.

county of Staffordshire where, between 1800 and 1813, he produced porcelain with printed chinoiserie and other patterns at a pottery at Lane Delph. The saucer-dish (56) bears a blue-printed pseudo-Chinese seal mark (GM 2545). Such marks should be examined very carefully before an attribution is made. The Miles Mason mark is very similar to that used on Coalport porcelain produced at the Caughley works between 1810 and 1815 (see p24). The Mason seal, however, is outlined by a single line; the Coalport seal has a double line.

The Mason business remained in the same family until 1854. In 1813 Miles Mason retired and the pottery was continued by his sons George Miles Mason (1789–1859) and Charles James Mason (1791–1856). Until 1829 the firm was known as G. M. & C. J. Mason when it became C. J. Mason & Co until 1844. Details of the family are given in a book by R. Haggar, *The Masons of Lane Delph* (1952).

The family is best known for stone china. When Miles Mason retired in 1813 Charles Mason, his son, at once took out a patent for ironstone china which contained slag from iron furnaces and which proved to be heavy, strong and durable. The brothers then impressed the mark MASON'S PATENT IRONSTONE CHINA on the wares made of this new material. Some of the ironstones were printed in blue. A *Two-man Willow Pattern* was produced identical with the design used by John Turner (see pp14–15). *The Chinese Dragon Pattern* (58) is very similar to that used by the Spode factory on porcelain (112). Other patterns (57 and 59) were probably derived directly from Chinese prototypes. *The Peonies and Birds Pattern* (59) has sometimes been called 'Blue Pheasants'.

Job Meigh of Hanley

Job Meigh established his business at the Old Hall Pottery, Hanley, c1805 and took his son into partnership in 1812, trading as Job Meigh & Son. Although Job Meigh died in 1817 the pottery appears to have continued under the same name until about 1835. It then became Charles Meigh. Blue-printed wares made up a considerable proportion of the output. A very attractive series was produced by Job Meigh & Son called 'Zoological Sketches' of which an example is illustrated (60). The realistic animals and birds are well designed by someone who had a knowledge of nature and could draw with flair and accuracy.

57 *(above left) G. M. and C. J. Mason*
Vase and Table Pattern (A)
(Courtesy: Mr and Mrs David Aliband)
Indented ironstone plate (c1813–25), in medium blue, with a pattern of flowers in which the central features are a vase and a table. The border has flowers and scrolls with a catherine wheel shading. Printed mark: MASON'S above a crown and drape which carries the words PATENT IRONSTONE CHINA (GM 2530).
Impressed mark: MASON'S PATENT IRONSTONE CHINA in one line (GM 2539).
Diam 8in. Narrow double foot rim. Colourless glaze on grey-blue ironstone.

58 *(above right) G. M. and C. J. Mason*
'Chinese Dragon' Pattern
Indented plate (1813–25), in light-medium blue, with a single Chinese dragon covering the face of the plate. The border carries a speckled serpent and other scroll motifs with the same scale-shading as the dragon's body.
Marks as for 57.
Diam 8in. Narrow double foot rim. Colourless glaze on grey-blue ironstone. Weight 11½oz.

59 *(below left) G. M. and C. J. Mason*
Peonies and Birds Pattern (A)
Indented plate (c1820–25), in light-medium blue, with peony flowers and exotic birds. The inner part of the border is packed with small catherine wheel scrolls to form a continuous band round the face of the plate. The rim portion is more open with geometrical motifs, flowers and scrolls.
Marks as for 57 and 58.
Diam 9.4in. Narrow double foot rim. Colourless glaze on white ironstone. Weight 18oz.

60 *(below right) Job Meigh & Son*
'Zoological Sketches': The Badger (A)
Indented plate (c1815–25) with moulded rim, in medium blue, with a badger in the centre. Around the central feature are flowers and scrolls with birds covering most of the rim and part of the face of the plate. A continuous scroll design encloses the overall pattern.
Printed mark: ZOOLOGICAL SKETCHES in rectangular panel against a background with a lion, and a bird in a tree. Below this pattern is the maker's mark in cursive letters: J. M. & S. (GM 2628).
Diam 4in. Double foot rim. Faintly rippled pale blue glaze on cream-coloured body.

John Meir of Tunstall

John Meir had a small pottery at Tunstall from c1812 and took his son into partnership sometime between 1836 and 1841 when it became John Meir & Son. The example illustrated (61) is of very fine quality indeed and the rippled glaze suggests that it was probably made before c1820. John Meir also made children's plates (Little, plate 43).

Books of ceramic marks sometimes refer to John Meir's premises in 1812 as the Greengates Pottery. In fact, Meir only took over Greengates in 1820 when Benjamin Adams ceased to operate there. This was part of an expansion programme. The firm of John Meir & Son continued until 1897.

The Wild Rose Pattern

This pattern, named after its border, came second only to the standard willow pattern in popularity between about 1830 and 1855. The example illustrated (62) was made at the Middlesbrough Pottery between 1834 and 1844. It has been described as a Staffordshire canal scene. Most examples are unmarked and the quality of the wares with this pattern varies. Hundreds of examples have been examined, among them pieces by the following potters (listed with the earliest production dates):

Barker, Samuel & Son, Don Pottery, Swinton. 1834+

Bell, J. & M. P. & Co Ltd, Glasgow Pottery. 1842+

Bourne, Baker & Bourne, Fenton, Stafford, c1830+ (see Little, plate 12)

Bovey Tracey Pottery Co, Devon. 1842+

Burn, Joseph & Co, Stepney Bank Pottery, Ouseburn. 1852+

Fell & Co, Newcastle. 1830+

Meir, John & Son, Tunstall, Staffs. c1840+ (see GI 396)

Middlesbrough Pottery (61). 1834+

W. R. Midwinter Ltd of Burslem. 1910+ (under the title 'Rural England')

Read, Clementson & Anderson, Shelton, Staffs. 1836+

Townsend, George, Longton, Staffs. 1850+

Twigg, J. & Co, Kilnhurst Old Pottery. 1839+

Wood, John & Co, Stepney Pottery, Ouseburn. 1877+

No doubt there were very many more. Most of the marked specimens bear the name of the pattern —*Wild Rose* or *Improved Wild Rose*. This pattern had already established itself as a popular line in the 1830s, before the Copyright Act of 1841.

61 (*above*) *John Meir   River Fishing Pattern* (A) *Indented dish (c1810–20), in dark-medium blue, with country scene showing two boys fishing in a river. Cows stand in the water, there is a mill, a wooden bridge, some timbered cottages, and a church spire in the distance. The border is of wild roses against a stippled ground.*
Impressed mark: MEIR (in small capitals) and 16. Length 16.8in. Width 13.1in. Prominent stilt marks. Pale blue rippled glaze.

62 (*below*) *Middlesbrough Pottery
'Wild Rose' Pattern
Indented dish (c1834–44), in dark blue, with a canal scene. Two pairs of men are in canal boats; there is a bridge and a cottage. In the distance is a church and a country mansion. The border is of wild roses against a cross-hatched background, dark at the edge and lighter towards the face of the dish.
Impressed mark: MIDDLESBRO' POTTERY arranged round an anchor. A blurred impressed figure below the anchor, either 10 or 40, and another figure 45 nearby.
Length 11.3in. Width 9.1in. No foot rim. Clear smooth glaze on speckled white body.*

Maddock & Seddon of Burslem

The chinoiserie patterns which appeared between 1820 and 1840 usually include rococo C-scrolls and English trees and flowers. The plate (63) made by Maddock & Seddon of Newcastle Street, Burslem, can be dated to between 1839 and 1842. The picture—not inappropriately called 'Fairy Villas'—is surrounded by a border of flowers and scrolls. The general impression is of lightness and delicacy compared with earlier chinoiserie.

Minton of Stoke

By 1796 the Minton factory was already sending pottery to London warehouses. Some went to Abbot & Newbury, some to Arthur Minton (Thomas Minton's brother) who had a large business in Swallow Street. In 1798 a china warehouse in Bath was added to the list and in the early years of the nineteenth century Chamberlain of Worcester, and Wedgwoods bought wares from Thomas Minton. The services were not marked though G. A. Godden in *Minton Pottery and Porcelain of the First Period, 1793–1850* (1969) illustrates two-man willow pattern tea services printed in blue which were supplied to Wedgwood in 1806 (plates 1 and 3). One of these is described as *The Nankin Temple Pattern*. By 1817 Thomas Minton's sons, Herbert and Thomas, had joined the business. Thomas Minton left in 1821 and soon after this date the first marked earthenwares appeared. The wares usually bear a cartouche with the name of the pattern. In 1836, after the death of Thomas Minton Sr, Herbert Minton formed a partnership with John Boyle and the marks of this period include a cursive *M & B*. But to return to the question of patterns. Most of Minton's earthenware of the 1822–36 period has the same lightness and delicacy as the plate and jug with *Chinese Marine* designs (64 and 65). The jug weighs less than 5oz and has a particularly attractive shape, typical of the 1830s.

There is a large Minton presentation jug dated 1828 printed with a *Chinese Scenery* pattern in the museum at Newbury, Berkshire.

The Bristol Pottery

The Temple Back Pottery, close to Temple Church in Bristol, was built by Edward Ward in 1683. For over a hundred years it made delftware. Then, in the 1780s, under the ownership of Joseph Ring it produced fine creamwares decorated with enamel colours by such artists at William Fifield. In 1813

63 (*above left*) Maddock & Seddon
'Fairy Villas' Pattern
Indented plate (c1840) with moulded edge, in medium blue, with ornate pagodas and a river with sailing boat. The border which descends to the well of the plate is profusely printed with flowers. A scrolled band defines the outer edge.
Printed mark: 'Fairy Villas' in cartouche with the maker's mark M & S below.
Diam 10in. Single foot rim. Smooth colourless glaze.

64 (*above right*) Minton
'Chinese Marine' Series Pattern
(*Courtesy: Mrs Elizabeth Carter*)
Indented plate (c1822–36) with gadrooned edge, in light-medium blue, with a Chinese scene with pagodas, and two men standing in an archway. Beyond lies the sea with distant ships. The border is of rococo scrolls and sprays of flowers.
Printed mark: 'Chinese Marine' in a scrolled cartouche above a cursive M. Below are the words OPAQUE CHINA.
Diam 10.3in. Double foot rim. Smooth colourless glaze on white body.

65 (*below left*) Minton
'Chinese Marine' Series Pattern
Fluted jug (c1822–36) with moulded decoration below spout and on handle, printed in medium blue, with a scene including a large temple and several small pagodas close to the sea with sailing ships flying pennants.
Printed mark as for 64.
Height to handle 4.3in. Flat foot rim. Smooth colourless glaze on white body.

66 (*below right*) Pountney & Goldney
'St Vincent's Rocks' Pattern
Indented plate (c1840), in dark-medium blue, with a view of St Vincent's Rocks, Bristol, with sailing ships and a rowing boat on the river. The picture is framed in a stringing of small scrolls and stylised leaves. The border pattern of flowers and swags suspended from rings has a stipple ground and extends into the well of the plate.
Impressed mark: POUNTNEY & GOLDNEY in horseshoe form around a cross (GM 3127).
Printed mark: ribbon with ST VINCENT'S ROCKS within a cartouche of leaves and scrolls.
Diam 10.1in. Double foot rim. Speckled body with many imperfections. 'Gritty' blue glaze.

John Decimus Pountney became a partner in the firm and in 1816 was operating the pottery with Edwin Allies. During this partnership the first blue-printed wares appeared, and they were also produced during the succeeding partnership of Pountney & Goldney (1836–49). Production became important after about 1830 when a 'Mr Wildblood' is said to have come from Burslem to be responsible for this side of the business.

Many of the patterns used were derivative but, as with the Herculaneum Pottery in Liverpool in the Case & Mort period, local topographical scenes were popular. The series title used by the Bristol Pottery was 'Views near Bristol'. A view of 'Bristol Hot Wells' by Pountney & Allies is illustrated by Little (plate 94). Other views were of the River Avon, of Cumberland Basin, Bristol, and of Bristol harbour and the ship *David* (which belonged to the pottery proprietors). The view of St Vincent's Rocks (66) bears the mark of Pountney & Goldney.

The derivative pieces explode the view that it is possible to recognise a maker from his border pattern. Compare *The Gothic Ruins Pattern* (67) of Pountney & Allies with Spode's *Girl at the Well Pattern* (116) produced at Stoke before the firm became Copeland & Garrett in 1833. The borders are identical and so are the trees and flowers in the central picture but the girl at the well has been cleverly replaced by the gothic ruins. Perhaps Mr Wildblood brought some Staffordshire designs with him for adaptation when he moved from Burslem to Bristol.

A series called *The Drama* leads to even more interesting speculation. This series was first produced by John Rogers & Son at Dale Hall, Longport (see pp60–2). A dish with a scene from *The Winter's Tale* (68) is impressed POUNTNEY & GOLDNEY, and Little illustrates a similar plate with a scene from *Midas* made by the same partnership. Rogers ceased to operate in 1836. Pountney & Goldney started in the same year. In the Rogers version one group of musical instruments in the border includes a mask (79); in the Bristol version (68) there are three small flowers.

Another Bristol dish illustrated by Little (plate 92) with the arms of the City of Bristol bears the same border as Riley's *Dromedary Pattern* (73) which was itself pirated by the Bristol Pottery (a plate apparently printed from worn plates, with the mark of Pountney & Goldney, is in the author's collection). Other designs pirated by this firm are noted elsewhere.

67 (above) *Pountney & Allies*

Gothic Ruins Pattern (A)
Eight-sided indented dish (c1830+), in light-medium blue, with a country scene of gothic ruins against distant mountains. To the right is a tree, to the left a large spray of leaves and flowers. The border of leaves and flowers descends towards the well of the plate.
Impressed mark: POUNTNEY & ALLIES *in horseshoe form around a cross and an impressed figure 12.*
Length 12.8in. Width 9.5in. No foot rim. Smooth colourless glaze.
(Examples of this pattern with the impressed mark of POUNTNEY & GOLDNEY *have been noted.)*

68 (below) *Pountney & Goldney*

'The Drama' Series:
Winter's Tale, Act 4, Scene 3
Eight-sided indented dish (c1840), in light-medium blue, with a country scene from Shakespeare. The words Winter's Tale, Act 4, Scene 3 are printed below the picture. The border of pale flowers against a stippled ground carries groups of musical instruments and theatrical accoutrements and descends towards the picture on the face of the plate.
Impressed mark: POUNTNEY AND GOLDNEY *arranged in horseshoe form around a cross (GM 3127) with an impressed figure 14.*
Printed mark: THE DRAMA *within a wreath.*
Length 14.5in. Width 11.2in. No foot rim. Very slightly rippled colourless glaze.

52

J. & W. Ridgway

John & William Ridgway of Cauldon Place and Bell Works, Shelton, Hanley, operated between about 1814 and 1830. They took over the firm which had been established by their father Job Ridgway in 1802 and which had been John Ridgway & Sons from 1808. The pottery had a thriving export business. Moore refers to Ridgways as 'one of the best-known names in America, anyway in connection with the much sought-after "old blue".' The firm certainly kept a high standard. A series of views of Oxford and Cambridge colleges has attracted much attention on both sides of the Atlantic because of its interest and quality. Each view is set in an eight-sided panel surrounded by a medallion border common to the series. Seventeen examples have been recorded of which two are illustrated. The series included:

Cambridge: Caius College
               Clare College
               King's College
               Library of Trinity College
               Pembroke Hall
               Senate House
               Sidney Sussex College (69)
               St Peter's College
               Trinity Hall
Oxford: All Souls' College and St Mary's Church
               Christchurch (see Laidaker, *Anglo-American China*, Part II, p64)
               Christchurch (a different view)
               Observatory
               Radcliffe Library (see Little, plate 51)
               Theatre Printing House (70)
               Trinity College
               Wadham College

It is probable that these views were specially drawn for the Ridgways. Moore regards the series as of superior quality to the 'Beauties of America' series by the same firm because of the 'better class of drawing they had to work from'. The American views have a border with rose medallions and include the following notable buildings:

Boston: Almshouse
             Athenaeum
             Court House
             Hospital
             Insane Hospital
             Octagon Church
             State House
             St Paul's Church

69 (above) *John & William Ridgway*
'Sidney Sufsex College, Cambridge'
Eight-sided indented dish (c1814–30), in dark blue, with a view of Sidney Sussex College, Cambridge, showing figures in the foreground playing bowls on the green. The picture is framed by white and dark-blue bands. The wide border which descends to the well of the dish shows trumpet-shaped flowers and four scrolled medallions with two themes —children feeding a goat and children milking a goat.
Printed mark: 'Sidney Sufsex College Cambridge' in cursive letters within a lozenge-shaped cartouche with the words OPAQUE CHINA within the upper border. Below the cartouche is the maker's name J. & W. RIDGWAY.
Length 14.6in. Width 9.4in. No foot rim. Slightly rippled very pale blue glaze.

70 (below) *John & William Ridgway*
'Theatre Printing House, Oxford'
Eight-sided indented dish (c1814–30), in dark blue, with a view of the Clarendon Building (ie The Printing House) and the Sheldonian Theatre with the tower of All Souls' College showing between them. The dish carries the series border (see 69 above).
Printed mark: 'Theatre Printing House &c Oxford' in cursive letters within a lozenge-shaped cartouche with the words OPAQUE CHINA within the upper border. Below the cartouche is the maker's name J. & W. RIDGWAY.
Length 18.6in. Width 14.2in. No foot rim. Slightly rippled blue glaze.

Charleston:	Exchange
Hartford, Conn:	Deaf and Dumb Asylum
Harvard:	College
New York:	Almshouse
	City Hall
Philadelphia:	Library
	Pennsylvania Heights
	Staughton's Church
Savannah:	Bank
Washington:	Capitol
	Mount Vernon

In each case the view is named on the base of the ware. The heavy stone china gadrooned dish (71) by J. & W. Ridgway bears the India Temple pattern; it could hardly provide a greater contrast though considerable quantities appear to have been made for the home market.

The plate with the view of *Osterley Park* (72) is simply impressed 'Ridgway' in small lower case letters. This mark does not appear to have been recorded but it is undoubtedly an early piece with a deep-blue rippled glaze and could have been made by Job Ridgway & Sons (c1808–14).

John & Richard Riley

John and Richard Riley established a pottery at Nile Street, Burslem, c1802, and moved to Hill Works, Burslem, in 1814 where they produced fine blue-printed ware until 1828. Richard may have died before the firm closed down.

The output was considerable. There are oriental scenes which usually carried a border of garden flowers. One of these is *The Dromedary Pattern* (73) which has much in common with the *Zebra* (80 and 81) and *Elephant* (82) patterns used by John Rogers & Son. Indeed, the border of Riley's *Dromedary Pattern* is exactly the same as that of Rogers's *Elephant Pattern*. The *Dromedary Pattern* was also used by Pountney & Goldney of Bristol (possibly using Riley's old copper plates) and the border was used with other Bristol patterns (Little, plate 92). Who would dare to attribute an unmarked plate from this border pattern?

71 (*above*) *John & William Ridgway*
'India Temple' Pattern
Six-sided gadrooned dish (c1814–30), in medium blue, with a scene which is described in the title as 'India Temple'. The temple is built on the edge of a promontory on which stands a three-storey building of pagoda-style. The ships in the estuary fly flags and pennants and the figures in the foreground suggest Far Eastern rather than Indian people. The picture is framed in a band of lines and scrolls. Between this and the gadrooned edge of the dish is a border with alternating bands of flowers and geometrical and scroll motifs.
Printed mark: INDIA TEMPLE STONE CHINA J. W. R. *within a shield (GM 3264).*
Length 14.4in. Width 12.5in. No foot rim. Slightly rippled colourless glaze on heavy stone china body weighing 3lb 6oz.

72 (*below left*) *Ridgway*
Osterley Park Pattern (A)
Dished indented plate (c1814–30), in dark blue, with a scene in Osterley Park. The mansion appears in the background (left). In the foreground is a bridge over a stretch of water with a group of resting fallow deer in the foreground. The trees include a willow. The border design is of flowers and leaves against a dark blue ground shading to a lighter stippled ground towards the inner band which separates the border from the central picture.
Impressed mark: Ridgway *(in lower case letters).*
Diam 9.9in. No foot rim. Rippled very blue glaze.

73 (*below right*) *John & Richard Riley*
Dromedary Pattern (A)
Dished indented plate (c1814–28), in dark blue, with an oasis scene showing date palms and the three pyramids in the distance. In the foreground a man with a staff holds a dromedary by a halter. Out of keeping with this scene is a dome-like structure supported on pillars. The wide border of flowers with dark blue leaves against a stipple ground descends to the well of the plate.
Printed mark: RILEY'S *on an oval buckled strap with the words 'Semi China' within (GM 3329).*
Diam 10in. Single narrow rounded foot rim. Greenish-blue rippled glaze.

The Eastern Street Scene Pattern (74) is known to be a composite picture rather than one based on a single engraving. This is a fine example of a piece in which a foreign scene has been given a typically English border of garden flowers which include the Sweet William.

Romantic scenes were used a great deal by the Rileys. The well-designed patterns (75 and 76) which have been given the titles of *The Europa Pattern* and *The Girl Musician Pattern* seem to belong to the same series though they carry different borders. It seems likely that the mounted bull and the figures in the foreground of the former are meant to represent the story of Europa, the daughter of the Phoenician King, Agenor (or in the Iliad, the daughter of Phoenix). Zeus was apparently overwhelmed by the beauty of Europa. He decided that he would assume the form of a tame bull and approached Europa and her maidens in this guise when they were sporting near the shore. Attracted by the gentleness of the creature, Europa mounted his back and he then swam with her to the Island of Crete. Unfortunately, it has not yet been found possible to find an equally convincing story to fit the scene of *The Girl Musician* plate.

The first blue-printed wares produced by John and Richard Riley were probably those with topographical scenes depicting country houses. They have a most striking border of flowers and large leafy scrolls. The example illustrated (77) has a printed mark on the back stating the locality—Denton Park, Yorkshire. The engraving is particularly fine. Examples with views of The Rookery, Surrey (now demolished), and of Bretton Hall, Yorkshire, have been noted and William Turner illustrates a jug with an Irish view of Gracefield, Queen's County.

Moore (p283) lists seven further views in the series under the name of 'J. W. Riley' (clearly an error). They are:

Bickley, Kent
Cannon Hall, Yorkshire
Goggerddan, Cardiganshire
(see J. K. des Fontaines, plate 139e)
Hollywell Cottage, Cavan
King's Cottage, Windsor Park
Kingsweston, Gloucestershire
Taymouth Castle, Perthshire

It seems likely that the Rileys exported wares printed with this series of views to America.

74 (above) *John & Richard Riley*
*Eastern Street Scene Pattern** (A)
Indented dish (c1810–28), in dark-medium blue, with an Eastern street scene (some features suggest the Near East, others the Far East). Beneath the tree on the left is a rectangular seat-like structure decorated on its sides with figures. Against the tree appears the puzzling bust of another figure. The border of flowers consists mainly of orchids and Sweet Williams.
Printed mark: RILEY'S on an oval buckled strap with the words 'Semi China' within (GM 3329).
Impressed mark: 12.
Length 12.7in. Width 10.4in. No foot rim. Rippled pale greenish-blue glaze.
*Note: This pattern is derived from two prints in T. and W. Daniell's *Oriental Scenery* (1796). It combines 'The Sacred Tree of the Hindoos at Gyah, Bihar' with 'A View of the Chitpore Road, Calcutta'.

75 (below left) *John & Richard Riley*
Europa Pattern (A)
Indented plate (c1810–28), in dark-medium blue, with a romantic scene of a lake, waterfall and distant buildings. The figures in the foreground are clearly intended to depict the story of Europa. The border of English flowers which includes the wild rose has a stipple ground shading from dark to a lighter blue towards the well of the plate.
Printed mark: as on 74.
Diam 10in. Rounded single foot rim. Rippled greenish-blue glaze.

76 (below right) *John & Richard Riley*
The Girl Musician Pattern (A)
Indented plate (c1810–28), in dark blue, with romantic scene of mountains, river, waterfall and country house. In the foreground a boy herdsman kneels before a girl playing a simple wind instrument with a second girl standing behind her. The border is of English flowers on a dark stippled ground which shades to a paler blue near the well of the plate.
Impressed mark: RILEY
Printed mark: as on 74 and 75.
Diam 10in. Rounded single foot rim. Rippled greenish-blue glaze.

Rockingham Works, near Swinton

The production of blue-printed wares began at this pottery c1806 when it was known as the Swinton Pottery under John and William Brameld. It became known as the Rockingham Works after 1826 when Earl Fitzwilliam had provided financial assistance. Operations ceased in 1842. Although there had been a close link with the Leeds factory before 1806 there is no evidence that blue-printed wares were made at the Swinton Pottery before that date; all those noted or recorded bear the name 'Brameld'. There is a marked example of a willow pattern in the Sheffield Museum and a *Woodman Pattern* (see Little, plate 99) was also used. Many of the wares show the results of poor workmanship with blurred printing and a poor glaze which tends to flake away. Although many examples of Rockingham wares have been examined, the only one that would merit a place in a collection, using quality as a criterion, is the plate (77) which bears *The Castle of Rochefort* pattern. Line engraving and stipple, with some cross-hatching, has produced a good 'depth' to the view and there is an attractive border. The title appears in a cartouche. This plate may well have been made in the 1810–20 period before the factory ran into financial difficulties. For a full history of this pottery see Eaglestone, A. A., and Lockett, T. A., *The Rockingham Pottery*, Rotherham 1964 (1973).

The Rogers Family

The name of Rogers ranks high so far as the production of blue-printed wares is concerned. Most pieces which bear the name are of good quality. The impressed mark ROGERS was used by John & George Rogers of Dale Hall, Longport, between 1784 and 1814 and also by the succeeding partnership of John Rogers & Son until 1836 when the pottery closed down. Nearly all their wares appear to have been clearly marked but there is no evidence that blue-printed wares were produced in the eighteenth century; most of them seem to date from about 1810. Between 1810 and 1836 the output must have been enormous. A wide range of patterns and shapes was produced, mainly for the home market though some special patterns were also designed for export to America.

Rogers' Drama Series

One interesting and unusual series produced in the second quarter of the nineteenth century was called *The Drama*. Each pattern represents a scene

77 (above) *John & Richard Riley*
        Country Houses Series:
        'Denton Park, Yorkshire'
Indented dish (c1810–28), in dark blue, with a view of Denton Park, Yorkshire, in parkland with deer. The picture is framed by a narrow wavy band, and the border of flowers, large scrolls and geometrical motifs against a cross-hatched ground descends to the well of the dish.
Printed mark: a ribbon twining around a branch carrying the words DENTON PARK, YORKSHIRE. RILEY.
Impressed marks: 8 and 14.
Length 14.6in. Width 11.8in. No foot rim. Colourless rippled glaze.

78 (below left) *Rockingham*
        'The Castle of Rochefort' Pattern
Indented plate (c1810–20), in medium blue, with a romantic scene showing a man with fishing rod walking with a lady carrying a basket. There is a river crossed by a two-arch bridge. On the left of the picture a waterfall cascades over a cliff and on the edge of the cliff beside the fall is the Castle of Rochefort. The border of scrolls and flowers has a net background.
Impressed mark: BRAMELD *in a small impressed cartouche.*
Printed mark: Castle of Rochefort, South of France in cursive letters within a cartouche.
Diam 10in. No foot rim. Pale greenish-blue rippled glaze.

79 (below right) *John Rogers & Son*
        'The Drama' Series: 'The Deserter, Scene 1'
Indented plate (c1814–36), in medium blue, with a view from the play 'The Deserter, Scene 1'. These words appear below the picture which shows a girl with a spinning-wheel at a cottage doorway, with a young soldier carrying a bundle on a stick standing before her. The border of pale flowers against a stipple background carries groups of musical instruments and theatrical accoutrements.
Impressed mark: ROGERS.
Printed mark: 'The Drama' in a wreath.
Diam 6.5in. Double foot rim. Smooth blue glaze.

 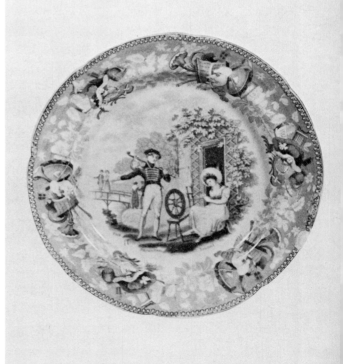

from a popular play or opera and the title with the details of act and scene is printed on the wares below the picture.

The Victoria and Albert Museum exhibits an impressed Rogers' plate (Little, plate 59) with a scene from *Love in a Village*, a ballad opera by Isaac Bickerstaffe (1735–1812), first performed at Covent Garden in 1762.

The *Drama* series includes scenes from:

As You Like It (two scenes); *The Deserter* (79); *Douglas; Two Gentlemen of Verona; Henry IV; Henry VI; Love in a Village; Loves Labour Lost; Maid at the Mill; Merchant of Venice* (two scenes); *The Merry Wives of Windsor; Midas; Much Ado about Nothing; The Quaker; The Revenge; The Taming of the Shrew* (two scenes); *The Tempest;* and *A Winter's Tale.*

Rogers' Animal Patterns

John Rogers & Son produced two interesting patterns with animals in an oriental setting. One is of an elephant in a garden with pagodas (82), not entirely inappropriate; the other (80 and 81) is of a zebra in a similar setting, hardly the right environment for a South African mammal. The border on *The Elephant Pattern* was also used by Riley on his dromedary pattern (72) and by Pountney & Goldney on the same pattern and also on a dish bearing the arms of the City of Bristol (Little, plate 92). G. A. Godden states that *The Elephant Pattern* was mentioned in an advertisement of 1818 (GI, plate 501).

The Zebra Pattern (80 and 81) was also used by Toft & May after 1826 (Little, plate 67). When Rogers' examples are compared with the Toft & May plate it is clear that there are certain differences in the engraved pattern. The Toft & May design shows more complicated decoration on the end of the building, the standing figure in black carries a staff, and there are distant mountains. The border has a lighter ground. But one has to look closely to pick out the differences. Was this a case of pirating, one firm from another? Or did an outside engraver sell two slightly different versions— one to each firm? The small tureen (81) shows how the border of *The Zebra Pattern* is made to predominate on a piece with this shape. The lion knob and lion-mask handles are typical of some Rogers' dinner wares (though not necessarily exclusive to them). These have been separately moulded and have been treated with a translucent blue glaze which reflects the light more brightly than the rest

80 (*above left*) *John Rogers & Son*
Zebra Pattern (A)
Indented dished plate (c1814–36), in medium blue, with a mounted zebra in an oriental garden with trees and pagodas. There are figures with a curving oriental head decoration. A key-pattern stringing separates the picture from a border of large flowers and dark leaves against a stipple ground.
Impressed mark: ROGERS *and* 6.
Diam 9.6in. Double foot rim. Pale greenish-blue rippled glaze.

81 (*above right*) *John Rogers & Son*
Zebra Pattern (A)
Sauce tureen (c1814–36) in which the border pattern is used for decoration, the zebra picture appearing only on the base inside the tureen. The handles and knob are moulded in the shape of a lion's head and covered with a translucent blue glaze.
Impressed mark: ROGERS.
Length of base 5.4in. Overall height 4.7in. Flat foot rim.

82 (*below left*) *John Rogers & Son*
Elephant Pattern (A)
Diamond-shaped dish (c1814–36), in medium blue, with an elephant in an oriental garden of trees and pagodas. The picture is framed in stringing which separates it from the border of flowers and dark leaves against a stipple ground.
Impressed mark: Rogers.
Length 7.1in. Pale blue glaze.

83 (*below right*) *John Rogers & Son*
Abbey Ruins Pattern (A)
Pierced tureen stand (c1814–36), with wavy edge, printed in medium blue with a scene showing the ruins of an abbey in a pastoral setting with cows. The picture is framed in a pierced band bounded on either side with moulded ropework, the piercing and moulding accentuated by thin lines of dark blue translucent glaze applied by hand. The two handles, each moulded in the shape of a single flower with leaves, have also been treated with dark blue translucent glaze.
Impressed mark: ROGERS.
Length 10.7in. Width 7in. Single foot rim. Thick blue glaze.

of the glazed surface. This special glazing is also seen on the tureen stand with *The Abbey Ruins Pattern* (83). This kind of handle for which a single flower with leaves has been moulded and glazed separately seems to be a characteristic feature of Rogers' wares. It occurs on a comport of roughly the same period (90 and 91) and was used on *The Drama* series (see J. K. des Fontaines, plate 145b). It has not been noted on the wares of other makers.

Rogers' Oriental Scenery Series

A series of scenes which correspond to Spode's Caramanian series show buildings, or the ruins of buildings, with some form of animal transport—a camel (84), horse (85) or draught-ox (86). These were designated *The Camel Pattern*, *The Musketeer Pattern* and *The Monopteros Pattern*, a name given to this scene by E. Morton Nance in *The Ceramics of Swansea and Nantgarw* (1942) p137. These scenes were, in fact, derived from T. and W. Daniell's *Oriental Scenery and Views in Hindoostan* published for T. Daniell by Robert Bowyer at the Historic Gallery, Pall Mall between 1795 and 1807. The Herculaneum Pottery, Liverpool used the same source for patterns.

Shortly after *The Monopteros Pattern* plate had been acquired a part-set of unmarked miniature pieces with the same pattern turned up in a saleroom (87). Since there is no evidence that the pattern was used by other potters it can be assumed that these small pieces were probably made by Rogers. This raises an interesting question. Were they traveller's samples or were they made as playthings for children—a 'dolly set' as it would be called today? In the days before there were many railways would salesmen carry a selection of large pieces? On the other hand, would a firm go to the trouble of making a considerable number of engravings to transfer-print a few samples? Perhaps these sets were made for both purposes. It is certain that in late Victorian times special 'dolly sets' were made for children but many of these are thicker, heavier and poorly potted.

It is sometimes stated that many pieces by Rogers are unmarked. What evidence is there to support this statement? The contrary would seem to be true. There is, however, one series attributed to Rogers which seldom appears to bear a mark. These are the splendid naval scenes in rectangular panels with a border of flowering shrubs and sea shells. S. Laidacker (Part II, p70) lists four such scenes: The Naval Fight between the Chesapeake and

84 (*above left*) *John Rogers & Son*
Gate leading to Musjed at Chunar Ghur Indented plate (c1814–36), in dark blue (*The Camel Pattern*). In the foreground a man is seen riding a camel and there are humped cattle at the water's edge. The picture has been designed to cover the whole plate and is separated from the edge by a narrow band of geometrical pattern 0.5in wide.
Impressed mark: ROGERS.
Diam 9.8in. Single foot rim. Pale blue rippled glaze.

85 (*above right*) *John Rogers & Son*
The Musketeer Pattern (A) Indented plate (c1814–36), in dark blue, with a classical scene in which long flights of steps lead to the buildings. Two musketeers, one mounted on a white horse, occupy the foreground. The picture has been designed to cover the whole plate and is separated from the edge by a narrow band of printed beading 0.5in wide.
Impressed mark: ROGERS.
Diam 8.4in. Single foot rim. Greenish-blue rippled glaze.

86 (*below left*) *John Rogers & Son*
Remains of an Ancient Building near Firoz Shah's Cotilla, Delhi (*Monopteros Pattern*) Indented plate (c1814–36), in medium blue, with a view of ruined buildings. A loaded draught-ox is being driven along a track in the foreground. There are two figures—one carrying a bundle on his head. The picture has been designed to cover the whole plate, though the flowers and trees are inappropriate to the arid country in the picture. The band at the edge of the plate is 0.5in wide.
Impressed mark: ROGERS.
Diam 10in. Single foot rim. Pale blue rippled glaze.

87 (*below right*) *John Rogers & Son*
Part of a miniature dinner service carrying the same pattern (see 86).

Shannon; Shannon; Landing Scene; Harbour Scene. Until a marked specimen is noted or recorded there must be some doubt about the attribution of this series to Rogers.

Sometimes the little printed marks which appear on blue and white earthenware are regarded as maker's marks. The sign of Mars (a circle with a small arrow) has been attributed 'fairly safely' to Rogers (Little, p95). This is certainly not a maker's mark though it may appear on Rogers' wares. It occurs on the wares of several potters. Spode pieces often carry it (see Williams, p209). These are workmen's marks, almost certainly the piece-rate tallies used by printers. A general warning is perhaps appropriate here about the acceptance, without question, of statements by earlier writers. Jewitt, writing in 1883, stated that John Rogers & Son were 'especially famed for their light blue "Broseley Dragon" and "Willow" pattern services'. This statement has been repeated by nearly every subsequent writer about blue and white earthenware. Yet is it true? The writer has searched in vain for some years for examples but without success though, in the process he has collected the fourteen Rogers' patterns illustrated in this book. If services of these 'Broseley' and 'Willow' patterns were 'famous', surely they should find their way into shops and salerooms much more frequently than they do.

The dinner services made by John Rogers & Son included some very large meat dishes with gravy wells, of which two examples are illustrated (88 and 89), the larger nearly 21in long. *The Fallow Deer Pattern*, which has a fine 'flowing' border, was given this name by Wedgwoods who used it at the end of the nineteenth century. (The pattern was printed in dark blue with the mark 'FALLOW DEER', WEDGWOOD, ETRURIA.) It seems reasonably certain that Rogers first introduced this pattern c1820.

The other large dish (89) is one of a series of English views which, unfortunately, do not carry printed titles. It is a view of Lancaster, very similar to one used by Herculaneum (see Smith, A. 'The Herculaneum China and Earthenware Manufactory, Toxteth, Liverpool', *Transactions of the English Ceramic Circle*, 7, Part I [1968], plate 29b).

Some makers made flat meat dishes which could be fitted with a pierced 'strainer' or 'mazarin' so that the juices could collect beneath. Examples may be seen on p111. It is likely that these were used mainly when serving boiled fish. The surplus water when the fish was transferred from the cooking

88 (*above*) *John Rogers & Son*

'*Fallow Deer' Pattern*
Large indented dish (c1814–36), in dark-medium blue, with a scene of fallow deer before a row of cottages. The cottages appear to be covered with snow. The trees on the left are without leaves; those to the right are in full leaf. The picture is framed in a stringing with small stylised leaves. The border of flowers seems to 'flow' round the dish on a stipple ground.
Impressed mark: ROGERS. Also an impressed figure 18 and letter B.
Length 18.8in. Width 13.6in. A foot rim 1in high raises one end of the dish so that meat juices can drain down shallow channels to a gravy well at the other end. Pale greenish-blue glaze.

89 (*below*) *John Rogers & Son*

View of Lancaster (A)
Large eight-sided indented dish (c1814–36), in medium blue, with a view of Lancaster. The large flowers of the border descend from the stipple ground of the rim towards the well of the dish.
Impressed mark: ROGERS. Also an impressed figure 20.
Length 20.8in. Width 15.9in. The dish stands on a rim 0.8in high at one end which slopes away towards the other end where there is a gravy well. Shallow channels arranged in herring-bone fashion drain the central well of the dish. Smooth pale greenish-blue glaze.

vessel to the strainer would drain into the dish. These strainers usually carry the pattern of the dish to which they are to be fitted though normally without the border pattern. They make excellent wall decoration.

The fruit comport (90) is a decorative piece which would grace any table. It has a deeply recessed base and the moulded blue-glazed handles described earlier (p64). One feature of the engraving deserves special notice. The colours range from a dark blue to a very light blue and it would appear that the perspective has been obtained by the use of a double transfer. The distant view of the gothic building has been printed in pale blue; this seems to have been overprinted with a foreground in darker blue. A similar technique has been used on a decorative dish described later (156–7).

Rogers' Classical Views

Two very different plates with classical views are illustrated as late examples of the Rogers factory (probably c1825–36). They both have a smooth glaze and bear a cartouche with the pattern name —a late feature. The example which is called *Tivoli* (92) is printed in a dark vivid blue quite unlike the colour used on other pieces from this factory. Very similar unmarked plates have been noted printed with a river scene and named *Ponte Rotto* in an exactly similar cartouche.

The *Athens Pattern* (93) is altogether lighter and has more in common with the Minton wares of the period (see page 50) than with other wares from the Rogers factory. *Athens* was used as the name for several different views.

Rogers and the American Market

There is no doubt that Rogers had an export trade to America but, unlike many other exporters, he does not seem to have issued many patterns with American subjects. The most notable is a view of Boston State House (94) which was a symbolic building for Americans at the time. Even in 1859 Oliver Wendell Holmes wrote of it as 'the hub of the solar system, you couldn't pry that out of a Boston man if you had the tire of all creation straightened out for a crowbar'. According to Moore, Rogers made three different engravings of the scene, including the one illustrated (94) with cows in the foreground 'almost identical with the view made by Stubbs but with a different border'.

90 (*above left*) *John Rogers & Son*
Gothic Pattern (A)
Fruit comport (c1830), seen from above, with wavy edge, printed in medium blue with a scene showing a gothic building in a country setting. An old man with a stick is talking to a woman sitting by the roadside. The dish carries the same floral border on rim and base. There are two handles each moulded in the shape of a flower with leaves and covered in dark blue translucent glaze.
Impressed mark: ROGERS.
Length 10.4in. Width 7.9in. Smooth colourless glaze.

91 (*above right*) *John Rogers & Son*
Gothic Pattern (A)
Side view of fruit comport shown in plate 90. The stem and base are hollow with a flat base rim. Height from base to rim 4.8in.

92 (*below left*) *John Rogers & Son*
'Tivoli' Pattern
Indented plate (c1825–36), in dark blue, with a view of classical ruins. The border of lilies, wild roses and other flowers is an integral part of the pattern and frames the picture.
Impressed mark: ROGERS.
Printed mark: 'Tivoli' in cursive letters with a rectangle surrounded by scrolls.
Diam 9.9in. Double foot rim. Pale blue rippled glaze.

93 (*below right*) *John Rogers & Son*
'Athens' Pattern
Plate (c1825–36) with indented, shaped edge, in medium blue, with a scene of classical ruins by a river from which fishermen in a boat are pulling a net. Wide border of flowers and scrolls which descends to the face of the plate. This is separated from the edge of the plate by printed beading.
Impressed mark: ROGERS.
Printed mark: ATHENS *on an eight-sided stippled panel.*
Diam 10in. Rounded foot rim. Smooth colourless glaze.

He was referring, of course, to Joseph Stubbs of Longport, c1822–35. Another Rogers' view has a chaise in the foreground.

J. & W. Ridgway, Ralph Stevenson & Williams, and Wood & Caldwell (Little, plate 76) all produced views of the State House, Boston.

Moore illustrates a Rogers' pitcher (fig 65) with a view of the Boston State House and writes that 'on the other side there is a view of the City Hall, New York'. Examples with these designs are greatly in demand and fetch high prices. Rogers' wares of many shapes printed with the Boston State House have been collected—dinner service and tea service pieces, pitchers, desk boxes, baskets, washbowls, soap dishes. S. Laidacker (Part I, p33) states that 'hundreds of pieces have been found in Italy'.

94 (*above*) *John Rogers & Son*

Boston State House
Indented dish (c1820), in dark blue, with a view of Boston State House and other buildings. In the mid-distance is a family group and a man pushing a covered barrow. Three cows occupy the foreground. The picture is framed by two thin blue lines and the border is of trailing flowers and leaves against a dark ground.
Impressed mark: ROGERS *with the impressed figure 11.*
Length 11.5in. Width 8.9in. No foot rim. Colourless rippled glaze.

Shorthose & Co of Shelton

The name Shorthose occurs in the title of several Staffordshire firms. The partnership of Shorthose & Heath of Shelton, Hanley, operated from c1795–1815 and appears to have been followed by Shorthose & Co from c1815–22. John Shorthose of Hanley (c1807–23) was probably connected with these firms (see GM, p576). The mark 'Shorthose & Co' on the saucer (95) could refer to any of the partnerships operating up to 1822. This tea bowl and saucer probably date from before 1815 since the pattern is a line engraving; there is no sign of stipple having been used. The practice of putting a band of colour on the rims of blue-printed wares was never common. Herculaneum and the Cambrian Pottery at Swansea sometimes used an ochreous colour and the Spode factory very occasionally touched up the face of their Greek pattern plates and dishes with red. No other factory, however, is recorded as having used a bright orange colour for the purpose.

A most interesting saucer with a printed mark 'Shorthose' shows a scene on the field of Waterloo with several armed soldiers in the uniform of the period. A building (possibly intended to represent the farmhouse used by Napoleon) is labelled WELLINGTON HOTEL WATERLOO.

95 (*below*) *Shorthose & Co*

One-man/insect Willow Pattern (A)
Tea bowl and saucer (c1815 or earlier) with a willow pattern with pagodas linked by a single-arch bridge on which one man faces to the left. Two men are seen in the doorway of the pagoda in the centre of the picture and a fourth man, with crook, in a doorway on the right. A fifth man steers a sailing boat with pennants. The willow tree appears to the left and there are two so-called 'apple' trees: the one in the foreground has provided an avalanche of windfalls. The geometrical border pattern carries an insect motif. The rims of both bowl and saucer are painted a bright orange colour over the glaze.
Printed mark on saucer: SHORTHOSE & CO.
Bowl and saucer have foot rims. The body, which is covered with a greenish-blue glaze, is light. The bowl weighs only 2½oz.

The Spode Works at Stoke-on-Trent

It is over a hundred years since Josiah Spode (1733–97) started to make earthenwares in Stoke after years of experience with other potters including Thomas Whieldon. He was one of the first potters in Staffordshire to make underglaze blue-printed wares (c1782) and before he died in 1797 he had established a thriving trade in this field. He was succeeded by his son, Josiah Spode II, who developed this trade and introduced a great variety of new patterns to an eager public because the Napoleonic Wars depleted supplies of Chinese porcelain; the ships that normally maintained trade with the east were required to take troops to Europe and to help blockade the coasts. In 1827, Josiah Spode II was succeeded by his son Josiah Spode III who died two years later. The firm was continued by W. T. Copeland who in 1833 acquired the business and formed a partnership with Thomas Garrett which endured until Garrett's retirement in 1847. The famous name of Spode was never dropped entirely and is still used today.

The blue-printed wares of Spode illustrated in the following pages were all produced before about 1830; the factory was already using other colours, notably green, when it came under the control of Copeland and Garrett. As a result of researches by S. B. Williams we know more about Spode's blue-printed wares than those of any other potter. Williams was a keen collector and published his *Antique Blue and White Spode* in 1942. The third and enlarged edition appeared in 1949.

Spode's Indian Sporting Series

Some of the most interesting dinner services produced by Spode were decorated with patterns derived from a publication by G. Orme of New Bond Street which appeared in monthly parts in 1805 under the title *Oriental Field Sports, Wild Sports of the East*. The text was by Captain Thomas Williamson and most of the aquatint engravings were by Samuel Howitt. In 1807 the material was published in two bound volumes but the illustrations were smaller. It was the discovery of a plate with the pattern *Chase after a Wolf* (96) which turned Williams into a collector. After giving Howitt full credit for his drawings he writes, '... the subsequent engravings used for the ware were really excellent and the blue colour of this service is as attractive as any blue used before or since'.

A single dinner service apparently used a num-

96 (above left) Spode   'Indian Sporting' Series: 'Chase after a Wolf'
Dished indented plate (c1810), in medium blue, showing a wolf running with a lamb in its mouth, chased by dogs and Indian hunters with spears or stones. The plate carries the typical Indian Sporting Series border.
Impressed mark: SPODE 5.
Printed marks: SPODE *and* CHASE AFTER A WOLF *in large capitals.*
Diam 9.6in. No foot rim. Slightly rippled pale blue glaze.

97 (above right) Spode   'Indian Sporting' Series: 'Death of the Bear'
Indented plate (c1810), in medium blue, showing hunters on horseback and on elephants with dogs, having hunted down a bear which they are killing with gunshot and spear.
Impressed mark: SPODE 44.
Printed marks: SPODE *and* DEATH OF THE BEAR *in large capitals.*
Diam 9.9in. No foot rim. Slightly rippled pale blue glaze.

98 (below) Spode   'Indian Sporting' Series: 'Hunting a Buffalo'
Tureen stand (c1810), in medium blue, with an Indian scene showing British hunters armed with guns, and Indian hunters with spears, mounted on elephants. They are hunting a charging buffalo. The picture is framed with a line of printed beading and the border consists of a series of animal scenes —a bear, a bird, a hog and a tiger all in their natural habitats.
Printed marks: SPODE *and* HUNTING A BUFFALO *in large capitals.*
Length 15.2in. Width 11in. Single deep foot rim. Rippled blue glaze.

ber of different patterns. Each bears its title in blue. These were almost certainly the first blue-printed wares to carry pattern titles. The following 'Indian Sporting' titles have been recorded:

Death of the Bear (97)
Driving a Bear out of sugar canes
Hunting a Buffalo (98)
Battle between a buffalo and tiger
Hunting a Kuttauss or Civet Cat
The Hog Deer at bay
The Hog at bay
Hog Hunter meeting by surprise a Tiger
The Dead Hog
Shooting a Leopard in a tree
Chasing a Tiger across a river
Chase after a Wolf (96)
Common Wolf trap (99 and 100)
Shooting at the edge of the jungle
Syces or grooms leading out Horses
Dooreahs, or dog keepers, leading out Dogs

All these patterns carry the same border. Some of them were certainly produced over a considerable period, if only as replacements. One example (100) bears the mark 'Copeland late Spode' which is usually regarded as having been used after 1847.

Williams (plates 3 to 36) illustrates all these patterns with the original engravings from which they were taken. J. & R. Clews used some of these patterns on American export wares. Some also bear a retailer's mark: 'John Greenfield, importer of china and earthenware, No 77 Pearl Street, New York'.

Spode's Caramanian Series

With the help of the British Museum staff, Williams was also able to trace the source of a series of patterns which are now referred to as Caramanian. They were based on engravings in the second of a series of volumes published by Luigi Mayer entitled: *Views in Egypt, Palestine and the Ottoman Empire* (1801–4). This dealt with 'views in the Ottoman empire chiefly in Caramania, a part of Asia Minor hitherto unexplored with some curious selections from the islands of Rhodes and Cyprus and the celebrated cities of Corinth, Carthage and Tripoli'. The series must have been produced at roughly the same period as the Indian Sporting series, or perhaps a little later. Quite inappropriately the patterns carry the Indian Sporting-style border. It was certainly on the market by 1809.

The titles are not printed on the wares but the following views have been recorded:

99 (above left) Spode   'Indian Sporting' Series: 'Common Wolf Trap'
Egg stand (c1810), in medium blue, with a scene —better seen on the plate (100)—showing a wolf trap over which a basket is suspended with a lamb. Above this is a pot from which water drips on to the lamb causing it to bleat. The noise has already attracted four wolves; one has plunged onto a rough cover of branches and leaves, below which is a deep well. The typical Indian Sporting Series border is carried twice in narrow bands inside and outside the rim.
Impressed mark: SPODE II.
Printed mark: SPODE.
Diam 7.3in. Height 2.2in. Rounded foot rim. Pale blue rippled glaze.

100 (above right) Copeland late Spode
    'Indian Sporting' Series: 'Common Wolf Trap'
This plate (c1850) shows the pattern clearly and indicates that production continued many years after it was first introduced.
Impressed mark: Small horse's head (0.2in) so far unrecorded, and figure 19.
Printed mark: Copeland late Spode (in lower case letters) and COMMON WOLF TRAP (in capitals) with the figure 10.
Diam 8.4in. No foot rim. Prominent stilt marks (3 x 3). Smooth colourless glaze.

101 (below) Spode   'Caramanian' Series: 'Triumphal Arch at Tripoli in Barbary'
Strainer (c1810), in medium blue, with a view of the Triumphal Arch at Tripoli built in the days when the Roman Empire extended into North Africa. There is a narrow scroll border.
Impressed mark: Spode (in lower case letters).
Length 16.4in. Width 11.8in.

An Ancient Bath at Cacamo (Coysh, 93)
The Castle at Boudron (Williams, fig 41)
Ancient Granary at Cacamo (Coysh, 91–2)
Necropolis or Cemetery at Cacamo (Coysh, 89)
Sarcophagi at Cacamo (Williams, fig 61)
Sarcophagi and Sepulchres at the Head of the Harbour at Cacamo (102)
Harbour Entrance at Cacamo (Williams, fig 45)
City of Corinth (Coysh, 88)
Citadel near Corinth (Coysh, 90)
Antique fragments at Limisso (Williams, fig 43)
The Harbour at Macri (Williams, fig 66)
Colossal Sarcophagus near Castle Rosso
Triumphal Arch at Tripoli in Barbary (101)

Spode's Italian Patterns

The Spode Italian pattern (103) can be regarded as the most commercially successful of all the patterns produced by the factory. According to a catalogue produced by W. T. Copeland & Sons for an exhibition in Oslo in 1966 it was first introduced 'c1795' though since stipple is freely used it seems more likely to have been first produced at least ten years later. It is thought to represent a scene in the Abruzzi district of Italy. It is still produced today and pieces can be found with the marks of Spode, Copeland & Garrett, Copeland late Spode, Copeland, and Copeland (England). Other makers copied this pattern. Marked specimens have been recorded by Zachariah Boyle of Hanley and Stoke, c1823–30 (Little, plate 13), John Mare of Hanley, c1800–25 (GI, plate 373), Pountney & Allies of Bristol 1816–35 (J. K. des Fontaines, p138), and Pountney & Goldney of Bristol, c1836–49 and a variant with floral border by Joseph Stubbs (1822–35).

Several Italian patterns used by Spode were taken from Merigot's *Views of Rome and its Vicinity* published in 1797–8. The dates given by Jewitt for the introduction of these patterns span thirteen years and must be regarded as unreliable. Williams considers it likely that they were produced before the Indian Sporting and Caramanian series. However, the Caramanian pieces bear the Spode mark in lower case letters and this is always regarded as an earlier mark than 'SPODE'.

These Italian patterns were almost certainly introduced between 1810 and 1820. In all there were four:

The Castle Pattern (104), often printed in a paler

102 (*above left*) Spode 'Caramanian' Series 'Sarcophagi and Sepulchres at the Head of the Harbour at Cacamo'
Plate, with twelve indentations in pairs (c1810), in medium blue, with a scene showing a number of figures standing, seated, or mounting steps, near several sarcophagi. There are two prominent palm trees, and in the distance some woodland. Birds fly in the sky. An interesting feature is the curious mask ornamentation on the wall and sarcophagi. Two animal heads protrude from the roof of the uppermost tomb. The border, from the Indian Sporting series, is separated from the central picture by a narrow band of S-scrolls.
Impressed mark: Spode (lower case letters) and 2.
Printed mark: The sign of Mars.
Diam 9.1in. No foot rim. Pale blue rippled glaze.

103 (*above right*) Spode 'The Italian Pattern'
Dished indented plate (c1816–20), in medium blue, with an Italian scene with classical ruins, a river, figures and domestic animals. The central picture is framed by a white dentil band beyond which a stippled area extends, overlapping the border pattern of flowers and scrolls.
Impressed mark: SPODE 15.
Printed mark: SPODE.
Diam 9.5in. No foot rim. Pale blue rippled glaze.

104 (*below left*) Spode 'The Castle Pattern'
Indented plate (c1810–15), in light-medium blue, with a view of the 'Gate of Sebastian' set among trees with a number of figures including a herdsman with three cows. The border has scroll, flower and leaf motifs and includes areas with a dark ground carrying fleur-de-lys motifs. A narrow castellated band separates the border from the central picture.
Impressed mark: SPODE 27.
Diam 9.8in. No foot rim. Pale blue rippled glaze.

105 (*below right*) Spode 'The Lucano Pattern'
Indented plate (c1810–15), in medium blue, showing the bridge of Lucano near Rome over which a herd of cattle is being driven. There are a number of birds flying in the sky, of which three are dominant. The border of wheat ears, vine leaves and grapes and olive branches against a line-engraved ground is separated from the central picture by a narrow unprinted band.
Impressed mark: SPODE 27.
Printed mark: SPODE.
Diam 9.5in. No foot rim. Pale blue rippled glaze.

76

blue than the three others, is based on Merigot's aquatint 'The Gate of Sebastian'.

The Lucano Pattern (105) shows the bridge of Lucano, 16 miles from Rome.

The Tower Pattern (107) shows the bridge of bridge of St Angelo, Rome. J. K. des Fontaines gives documentary evidence to suggest that the date of introduction for this pattern was 1811–12 (p137).

The Tower Pattern (107) shows the bridge of Salaro. The pattern has been revived by the Spode factory several times.

Each of the Merigot Italian patterns carries a distinctive border. A pattern or border alone on an unmarked specimen, however, is not sufficient evidence to attribute a piece to Spode. Other potters used these designs.

The Castle Pattern was used by the Cambrian Pottery at Swansea: examples have been noted with the marks of Bevington & Co, c1817–24 (GM 3767) and Dillwyn, after 1824 (GM 3769) suggesting that the design may have been used over a considerable period—c1817–50. According to Williams (pp96–7) it was also used by Baker, Bevans & Irwin at the Glamorgan Pottery, Swansea (1813–38) and by James & Ralph Clews of Cobridge, Staffordshire (1818–34).

The Lucano Pattern was used by Dillwyn of Swansea between 1824 and 1850 (GM 3769) and also by William Baddeley of Hanley before the firm closed down in 1822. These bear the impressed mark EASTWOOD (GM 202). E. Morton Nance, in his *Pottery and Porcelain of Swansea and Nantgarw* (1942), states that the Lucano pattern was also used 'at Bristol by the Pountney firm' (p153). Examples have also been recorded with the impressed mark of DONOVAN, the Dublin china dealer.

The border of *The Tower Pattern* was used on wares made by Sewell of St Anthony's Pottery, Newcastle-upon-Tyne (J. K. des Fontaines, plate 137e).

There is one more Italian pattern which may well have been used solely on tea services, for no dinner wares have been noted decorated in this way. Williams calls it the *Italian Church Pattern* (108). He suggests that it might represent 'Possagno and the church of the village where Canova was born and possibly buried, much visited by tourists about the time of his death, in 1822'. This has not, however, been confirmed.

106 *(above) Spode* 'The Tiber Pattern'
Dish (c1812), in medium blue, with a view of the River Tiber with the Castle of St Angelo (right), Trajan's column and St Peter's. Figures occupy the foreground and the setting of rocks, river bank and trees extends beyond the well of the dish to the rim. The border with a chain motif (only 0.5in wide) extends around the edge of the rim.
Impressed mark: SPODE 18.
Length 14.9in. Width 11.3in. No foot rim. Pale blue rippled glaze.

107 *(below left) Spode* 'The Tower Pattern'
Dished indented plate (c1812–15), in medium blue, with a view of the bridge of Salaro. Two fishermen with a net are on the river bank near the bridge and three birds figure prominently in the foreground. The border of two types of flower against a stipple ground is separated from the central picture by a narrow band with a leaf motif.
Impressed mark: SPODE 27.
Printed mark: SPODE.
Diam 9.8in. No foot rim. Pale blue rippled glaze.

108 *(below right) Spode*
'The Italian Church Pattern'
Saucer (c1820) with a wavy edge, printed in blue, with a view of an unidentified Italian church with a man, woman and child in the foreground. The picture is framed in a dentil band which separates it from a border composed of a garland of flowers threaded through six rings against a stipple ground. The outer edge of the border repeats the dentil band.
Printed mark: SPODE.
Diam 5.5in. Rounded foot rim. Smooth pale blue glaze.

Spode's Chinoiseries

A considerable number of willow patterns were produced between the first *Caughley Willow* (see p11) and the Spode *Standard Willow Pattern* (109). A catalogue of Spode-Copeland wares issued in connection with an exhibition in Oslo in 1966 states that 'it is believed that this famous pattern was introduced by Spode'. It also says that the Spode standard willow 'shows great technical advance in engraving with more use made of the stipple technique'. Spode had already produced other willow patterns which are illustrated and discussed by Williams (pp129–48). The standard willow pattern appears to be later than the others and could hardly have been introduced before about 1810. It could well have been even later. The possible reasons for its sudden popularity among potters in the 1820–40 period are referred to on p42 where a Herculaneum example is discussed.

It is almost impossible to attribute unmarked specimens of the standard willow pattern to a particular factory. The number of so-called 'apples' has no significance, as some writers would suggest. The engravers varied the number with the shape of the article. The Spode plate (109) has 32 apples. A Spode fruit dish with the same pattern has been noted with 74 apples and a Spode strainer in the author's collection has 92!

Other Spode patterns derived from Chinese sources. These include *The Bird and Grasshopper Pattern*, *The Lange Lijsen Pattern*, *The Chinese Dragon Pattern*, *The India Pattern* and *The Net Pattern*. The Bird and Grasshopper Pattern (110) appears to have been used exclusively on stone china, a body that was introduced in 1805. Williams describes a plate with the impressed mark SPODE'S NEW STONE and shows a Chinese dish (fig 127) from which the pattern was directly derived. He expresses the view 'that because this is practically an exact copy, one is led to assume that Spode's pattern was expressly made to replace breakages in the Chinese imported services'. However, Spode plates and dishes with this pattern are by no means uncommon; some full dinner services must surely have been made. *The Lange Lijsen Pattern* (111) was also derived directly from a Chinese design used in the Chien Lung period (Williams, fig 109) but in this case is printed on the usual pearlware body used for most Spode dinner services. *Lange Lijsen* is a Dutch name for 'slender damsel' sometimes corrupted in this country to become 'Long Elizas'. The pattern has also been called *The Jump-*

109 (*above left*) Spode   *Standard Willow Pattern* Indented plate (c1810–25), in medium blue, with the standard willow pattern with pagoda, fence in foreground, three men on a three-arch bridge and two large birds in the sky. The picture is framed in a band of geometrical motifs with small flowers and scrolls.
Impressed mark: SPODE 15.
Printed mark: SPODE.
Diam 9.9in. No foot rim. Pale blue rippled glaze.

110 (*above right*) Spode
                 'Bird and Grasshopper' Pattern Dished indented plate (c1805–15), in dark blue, with a Chinese flower and fence pattern with a bird and a grasshopper. The central picture is framed in a band of catherine wheel scrolls. The border has geometrical and flower motifs with Chinese writing scrolls and insects.
Printed mark: SPODE across a square pseudo-Chinese seal mark with the words 'Stone China' beneath.
Diam 9.5in. Sharp double foot rim. Colourless rippled glaze on heavy pale grey stoneware body weighing 18.5oz.

111 (*below left*) Spode   *'Lange Lijsen' Pattern* Indented plate (c1810–20), in medium blue, with a picture of a tall Chinese maiden and a short man or boy under an overhanging tree before a two-arch bridge. The picture is framed by a double band of decoration. This is bounded by a stipple band which fades into the wide border consisting of alternate panels showing pairs of maidens beneath a tree and flowering hawthorn respectively. They are divided by geometrical motifs.
Impressed mark: SPODE 27.
Printed mark: SPODE.
Diam 9.7in. No foot rim. Slightly rippled colourless glaze.

112 (*below right*) Spode
                 'Chinese Dragon' Pattern Plate (c1815), in dark blue, with an all-over pattern of Chinese dragons.
Printed mark: SPODE.
Diam 7.0in. Foot rim. Colourless glaze on smooth white porcelain body.

ing Boy. The Chinese Dragon Pattern (112) was used only on porcelain. It is not unlike *The Chinese Dragon Pattern* (58) used by G. M. & C. J. Mason.

The India Pattern (113) presumably got its name from the East India Company which imported the Chinese prototypes from which these Spode chinoiserie patterns were derived. It is a near copy of a design used in the K'ang Hsi period (1662–1772) and Williams illustrates a plate with this Chinese pattern (fig 116). He has recorded a Spode *India Pattern* plate (fig 118) which is dated August 1816. It bears the printed inscription: 'This piece of BLUE WARE is printed from CALX of British COBALT produced from Wheal Sparnon Mine in the County of Cornwall'. *The Net Pattern* (114) was made by the Herculaneum factory in Liverpool as well as the Spode factory and there is no clear evidence to decide the originator. Specimens vary only in small details. (Unmarked pieces have been noted with the edges painted in a yellow ochre colour, suggesting Herculaneum.) The Spode factory used this pattern well into the Copeland & Garrett period. It is possible that other potters may also have used *The Net Pattern*. A plate in the author's collection bears the printed initials CT, possibly the mark of Charles Tittensor of Shelton (c1815–23).

Spode's Greek Patterns

The plate (115) with a central design of a chariot drawn by four horses presents some interesting problems. It bears an impressed 'Spode' mark in lower case letters, normally regarded as an early mark. The colour is very deep blue, unlike Spode's other printed wares, and the edge of the plate and the lines which outline the central picture and the medallions are painted over the glaze with red enamel. Williams illustrates three Greek designs (figs 143–5) and expresses the view that they correspond to the 'Etruscan' pattern mentioned by Jewitt as an 1825 introduction. Yet everything about the plate suggests a much earlier date. Similar wares with Greek designs were made by other factories, notably Herculaneum, and examples printed in very light blue have also been noted. The attribution of an unmarked specimen is discussed on p100.

Spode's Floral Patterns

The Girl at the Well Pattern (116) may be regarded essentially as a floral pattern. It carries the same border as *The Union Spray Pattern* and must

113 (*above left*) Spode   'The India Pattern'
Indented plate (c1815–20), *in dark blue, with a pattern of flowering shrubs and insects framed in a wreath of leaves. The border is composed of eight panels with four distinct floral designs, each on a geometrically-designed ground.*
Impressed mark: Spode.
Diam 9.9in. No foot rim. Very pale blue rippled glaze.

114 (*above right*) Spode   'The Net Pattern'
Indented plate (c1810–15), *in medium blue, with a central circular design with a sunflower-and-insect motif forming a cross against a net background. This is framed in a narrow band of scrolls and flowers. The rest of the well of the plate is covered by four chinoiserie medallions with pagodas, all different, set in a pattern of flowers and leaves against a line-engraved ground. The border repeats the central framing band which is broken by four small chinoiserie medallions. It also includes leaves, flowers and geometrical motifs.*
Impressed mark: SPODE 30.
Printed mark: SPODE.
Diam 9.8in. No foot rim. Smooth colourless glaze.

115 (*below left*) Spode
     The Greek Pattern 1: The Chariot (A)
Indented plate (c1805–25), *in a dark blue, with classical scenes. The central picture shows a chariot with four horses, driven by a figure with lightning in his right hand. The border has four medallions and four vases each with a different scene, all against a leaf-and-berry ground. The lines which define the medallions and vases have been painted in red over the glaze.*
Impressed mark: Spode 3.
Painted mark overglaze: 1310.
Diam 10in. No foot rim. Rippled blue glaze.

116 (*below right*) Spode
     'The Girl at the Well' Pattern
Indented plate (c1820–30), *in medium blue, with a picture of a girl filling a ewer from a well. To the right is a tree, to the left a large spray of leaves and flowers. The border of trailing leaves descends to the well of the plate but is separated from the picture by an unprinted area.*
Impressed mark: SPODE 15.
Printed mark: SPODE.
Diam 9.8in. No foot rim. Pale blue rippled glaze.

have been produced in considerable quantities, for examples are by no means uncommon. The design was probably pirated by other makers; several unmarked examples have been noted with features that do not correspond with marked Spode pieces—one has a prominent foot rim, for example. A good quality tureen, well printed with *The Girl at the Well Pattern*, was marked with an underglaze blue-printed title—THE FONT—below a playing fountain. The firm of Pountney & Allies of Bristol adapted the pattern for its own purposes by replacing the girl by a gothic ruin (see 67).

The Union Spray Pattern (117 and 118) has been so named to differentiate it from *The Union Wreath Pattern* (Williams, fig 159). It has the same border as *The Girl at the Well Pattern* and the central spray includes rose, thistle and shamrock. L. Jewitt in *The Ceramic Art of Great Britain* (1883) mentions two 'Union' patterns, one introduced in 1822 and the *Union Wreath* in 1826. J. K. des Fontaines illustrates (plate 146b) a dish with the *Union Spray* made for the 59th Regiment of Foot, the Northamptonshire Regiment, which also uses the rose, thistle and shamrock in the border pattern. It is interesting to note that the *British History* series of Jones & Son (pp44–5) has a border with rose, thistle and shamrock of roughly the same period, c1826–8.

Spode's *Botanical Patterns* (119–20) show sprays of flowers against a shaded ground. The central spray has a line-engraved ground and the border a stipple ground. Williams illustrates a third pattern of this type (figs 150 and 152) and J. K. des Fontaines a fourth (plate 149f). There are also a number of other floral patterns with a white ground including *The Blue Rose Pattern* (Williams, figs 148, 154–5 and 157). One of these, described by J. K. des Fontaines as *The Chrysanthemum Pattern* (plate 142c), has a central picture of flowers and leaves and a border of flowers and scrolls. The border appears on a ridged stand with a central picture of a beehive and four bees (122). This must surely have been a stand for a honeypot, possibly part of the larger service.

The Filigree Pattern (121) used by Spode owes something to the Chinese influence but is, nevertheless, essentially English in character with its baskets of garden flowers. According to Jewitt it was introduced in 1823. It was used well into the Copeland & Garrett period.

This pattern was also used by Thomas Dimmock & Co (c1828–59). A tureen has been noted with the monogram mark of this firm (GM 1300).

117 (*above left*) Spode
The Union Spray Pattern (A)
Indented plate (c1820–30), in medium blue, with a spray of flowers held together by a ribbon. The spray includes the rose, thistle and shamrock. The border is of trailing leaves and flowers. A wide unprinted area lies between the face pattern and the border.
Impressed mark: SPODE 27.
Printed mark: SPODE.
Diam 9.8in. No foot rim. Colourless, very slightly rippled glaze on white body.

118 (*above right*) Spode
The Union Spray Pattern (A)
Small ewer (c1820–30), in medium blue, with a pattern of flowers held together by a ribbon (as in 117). The handle carries a pattern of grapes, vine leaves and tendrils, on a stipple ground.
Printed mark: SPODE.
Height 8in. Foot rim. Smooth glaze, tinged with blue, on a white body.

119 (*below left*) Spode
Botanical Pattern: Version 1 (A)
Plate (c1820) with twelve indentations, in medium blue, with a floral pattern, possibly of double narcissi, on a line-engraved ground, the border also of flowers on a stipple ground. A band separates the two and the outer edge of the border has intertwined bands.
Impressed mark: SPODE 30.
Printed mark: SPODE.
Diam 9.9in. No foot rim. Colourless glaze on white, rather heavy, body. Weight 14¾oz.

120 (*below right*) Spode
Botanical Pattern: Version 2 (A)
Dished plate (c1820), with twelve indentations, in medium blue, with a floral pattern on a line-engraved ground, the border also of flowers on a stipple ground. A band separates the two and the outer edge of the border has intertwined bands.
Impressed mark: SPODE 30.
Printed mark: SPODE.
Diam 9.9in. No foot rim. Colourless glaze on white, rather heavy, body. Weight 15oz.

Andrew Stevenson of Cobridge

The Filigree Pattern (123) attributed to Andrew Stevenson (c1816–30) is so much like the Spode Filigree Pattern (121), though differing in detail that one must surely have been based on the other, or the two versions may have come from the same engraver's workshop. The attribution to Andrew Stevenson must be treated with caution. It is based solely on the fact that the mark contains a three-masted ship similar to one which actually bears the name 'Stevenson' (see GM 3700 and 3702).

Most wares by Andrew Stevenson are printed in a dark blue. The Gothic Ruins Pattern is a good example. It is interesting to note that the medallions in the border are framed in scrolls identical with those used by William Mason of Lane Delph, c1811–15 (see GI, plate 389). J. K. des Fontaines illustrates an unmarked plate with The Gothic Ruins Pattern which he attributes to William Mason because there are 'existing marked specimens'. This would appear to be another case where two potters used the same pattern. Andrew Stevenson, like his brother Ralph Stevenson (c1810–32), had a large export trade to America and he used portrait medallions on the borders of some of his export wares with likenesses of Clinton, Jefferson, Lafayette and Washington. Some of his American views were drawn by W. G. Wall, a Dublin artist who is said to have visited America in 1818 to sketch some of the prominent buildings in New York including the Catholic Cathedral, City Hall and City Almshouse. In all some sixteen of Andrew Stevenson's American views have been recorded, mainly designed by Wall (see Moore, p259).

Interesting facts have recently come to light in connection with The Gothic Ruins Pattern which has now been identified as Netley Abbey. A plate with this pattern has been noted with the mark of a three-masted ship (GM 3700) without the enclosing ellipse. This mark can now be attributed fairly confidently to Andrew Stevenson. The author has recently examined a bowl in the Greenock Museum which has a mark with a three-masted ship associated with the words CLYDE POTTERY. This ship carries full sail and is *very different* from the mark attributed to A. Stevenson. It is the mark described by J. Arnold Fleming in *Scottish Pottery* (1923, p211) as 'of a ship inside a narrow oval garter'.

Andrew Stevenson also produced an English series with views of country houses and castles which was also exported to America. Some views in

121 (*above left*) Spode   'The Filigree' Pattern
Indented plate (c1825), in medium blue, with a central basket of flowers framed by a circular band of flowers and leaves. The remaining area is occupied by a wide border divided into six panels with sprays or baskets of flowers; the intervening areas are decorated with small flowers and scrolls.
Impressed mark: SPODE.
Printed mark: SPODE.
Diam 9.8in. No foot rim. Smooth colourless glaze.

122 (*above right*) Spode   The Beehive Pattern (A)
Stand (1820–30) with gadrooned edge, printed in the centre in medium blue with a beehive and four bees. A rim separates this from the border of flowers and scrolls.
Impressed mark: SPODE 39.
Printed mark: SPODE.
Diam 7.5in. Prominent rounded foot rim. Smooth pale blue glaze.

123 (*below left*) Attributed to Andrew Stevenson
'The Filigree' Pattern
Dished indented plate (1816–30), in medium blue, with a central basket of flowers framed by a circular band of flowers and leaves. The remaining area is occupied by a wide border divided into six panels with sprays of flowers, the intervening areas decorated with flowers against a stipple ground.
Printed mark: a three-masted ship above which the words SEMI-NANKEEN CHINA on a ribbon are surmounted by a crown, a thistle and a rose (GM 3702). There is a workman's mark in the shape of a clover leaf.
Diam 9.9in. Wide double foot rim. Deep blue rippled glaze.

124 (*below right*) Andrew Stevenson
Gothic Ruins Pattern (A)
Indented plate (c1816–30), in dark blue, with ruined gothic arches overgrown with trees and shrubs. A shepherd rests on his stick among a flock of sheep. Birds fly in the sky. The picture is framed by a narrow decorative band. The border of flowers and scrolled medallions with river and marine scenes has a stipple ground.
Impressed mark: A. STEVENSON STAFFORDSHIRE WARRANTED *between concentric circles surrounding a crown (a variant of GM 3701).*
Diam 8.3in. Double foot rim. Deep blue rippled glaze.

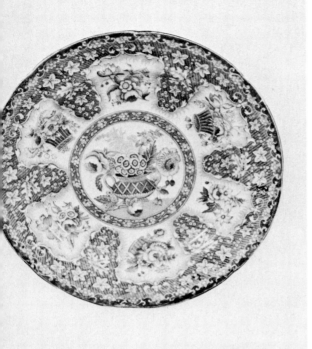

the series have medallion portraits of Washington and Clinton but most of them have a border of roses and other flowers as on the plate (125) with a view of Culford Hall, Suffolk. It is not wise to use the printed mark alone for attribution purposes since a similar mark was also used by Hackwood of Hanley c1830–40 (GM 1862). The following views in the Andrew Stevenson series have been recorded: Ampton Hall, Suffolk; Audley End, Essex; Barrington Hall; Boreham House, Essex; The Chantry, Suffolk; Culford Hall, Suffolk; Dulwich College, Essex; Enville Hall, Staffs; Felix Hall; Foulkbourn Hall (used with four different borders); Haughton Hall, Norfolk; Kidbrook, Sussex; Mereworth House; Oatlands, Surrey; Summer Hall, Kent; Tunbridge Castle, Surrey; Walsingham Priory, Norfolk; Wanstead House, Essex; Wolvesley Castle; Writtle Lodge (two versions). See Moore, N. H., *The Old China Book* (1935), p259.

Joseph Stubbs of Longport

Joseph Stubbs operated a factory at Dale Hall, Longport, Burslem, c1822–35, and between 1828 and 1830 worked with a partner as Stubbs & Kent. The wares were printed in dark blue (126) and there was a considerable export to America. S. Laidacker describes *The Peach and Cherry Pattern* as 'one of the most popular of all patterns in dark blue' (Part II, p81). Some services carried American scenes of which fifteen have been recorded including Boston State House, New York City Hall and the Upper Ferry Bridge, Philadelphia. Little illustrates a plate (fig 66) with a view of Fair Mount, near Philadelphia.

The Swansea Potteries

There were two potteries operating in Swansea early in the nineteenth century: the Cambrian Pottery (c1783–1870) which started to make blue-printed wares in the eighteenth century, and the Glamorgan Pottery which was owned by Baker, Bevans & Irwin (1813–38). The Cambrian Pottery was operated by Lewis Weston Dillwyn and his son until 1850 except for a period (1817–24) when it was let to T. & J. Bevington. This potworks established a trade with the West Indies; copper ore from Cuba came to Swansea docks and pottery provided a useful item in the return cargo.

125 (*above left*) *Andrew Stevenson*
'English Views' Series: 'Culford Hall, Suffolk' Indented plate (c1816–30), in dark blue, with a view of Culford Hall, Suffolk. Figures stand in the foreground, a church tower shows among the trees and heavy clouds fill the sky. The picture is framed by a narrow white dentil band. The border of wild roses and other flowers has a stippled ground, dark near the rim and lighter in colour towards the well.
Impressed mark: A. STEVENSON STAFFORDSHIRE WARRANTED *between concentric circles which enclose a crown (a variant of GM 3701).*
Printed mark: CULFORD HALL, SUFFOLK *on a cloth draped before a lidded urn with a background of leaves and shrubs.*
Diam 10.3in. Double foot rim. Three prominent single stilt marks on face. Rippled greenish-blue glaze.

126 (*above right*) *Stubbs & Kent*
Peach and Cherry Pattern (A)
(*Courtesy: Hampshire County Museum Service, No 238 in Bignell Collection Catalogue, 1943*).
Indented plate (c1828–30), in dark blue, with a circular pattern of fruit and flowers on a net ground. Decorative stringing separates it from a floral border with three large scrolled panels separated by single flowers on a lighter ground.
Impressed mark: STUBBS & KENT, LONGPORT *between concentric circles which contain a star-shaped device (GM 3730).*
Diam 9in. Double foot rim. Pale blue rippled glaze.

127 (*below left*) *Swansea: Cambrian Pottery*
Cockle and Whelk Pattern (A)
Small indented cockle plate (c1830–40) with a pattern of cockle and whelk shells.
Impressed mark: DILLWYN.
Diam 4in. Double foot rim. Smooth faintly blue glaze.

128 (*below right*) *Swansea: Glamorgan Pottery*
'The Ladies of Llangollen' Pattern
Sauce-tureen stand (c1813–20), in dark-medium blue, with a country scene of a castle, windmill, watermill and village. Two horsewomen, riding side-saddle, approach a man with scythe and firkin. Decorative stringing frames the picture. The border is of flowers and fan-like motifs.
Impressed mark: Prince of Wales feathers.
Printed mark: 5.
Length 7in. Width 5.5in. No foot rim. Pale blue rippled glaze.

The word SWANSEA may be seen on the wares of both the Swansea factories. The unusual small plate (127) with *The Cockle and Whelk Pattern* was made by Dillwyn's for use on the cockle stalls in Swansea market. The small oval tureen stand (128) bears the mark of the Glamorgan Pottery, in this case an impressed Prince of Wales feathers, a mark which is sometimes accompanied by the impressed mark of the maker, curved around the feathers, BAKER, BEVANS & IRWIN, SWANSEA. Little considers this to be a copy of a Cambrian Pottery pattern known as the *Ladies of Llangollen Pattern*. These two ladies were the Rt Hon Lady Eleanor Butler, daughter of the Marquis of Ormonde, and Miss Sarah Ponsonby, daughter of Viscount Duncannon, eldest son of the Earl of Bessborough. They were very great friends and very independent. One day they ran away from the house of their mutual cousin in County Kilkenny, crossed the Irish Sea and settled in Wales in a house called Plas Newydd at Llangollen. The wares decorated with this pattern are of good quality and most attractive. This is not so, however, with all the Glamorgan Pottery wares. The ewer (129) with the *Archers Pattern* is poorly decorated with a rather blurred transfer, either badly engraved or from worn plates.

John Turner of Lane End

John Turner of Lane End, Longton, was one of the first potters in Staffordshire to make blue-printed wares (see pp14–15). He produced a number of patterns on pearlware but no records seem to exist which describe his blue-printing on creamware (130 and 131). These have a strong blue glaze on a moulded cream-coloured body giving an overall impression of ivory. These patterns may well have been engraved by William Underwood, the 'blue printer' from Worcester who is said to have joined John Turner at Lane End in the 1780s and to have lived to 'a very advanced age'. *The Floral Pattern* (130) is remarkably like some of the painted patterns on Worcester porcelain. The design on the dish (131) has been called *The Villager Pattern* on the assumption that it may have been the pattern referred to by this name when the engraved copper plates from the Turner factory were sold in 1829 (see Hillier, p75).

129 (*above left*) Swansea: Glamorgan Pottery
'The Archers' Pattern
Ewer (c1830–8), in medium blue, with a scene showing a castle on the bank of a river which is spanned by a two-arch bridge. A lady and gentleman stand with bows and arrows, presumably to shoot the stag and doe in the middle distance. The border of C-scrolls and flowers includes pairs of peacock feathers tied together with ribbon. The handle is printed with a 'fibre' motif.
Impressed mark: BAKER, BEVANS & IRWIN curved around an impressed figure 7.
Printed mark: oval cartouche with the word 'Archers' with an arrow and quiver.
Height 8.8in. White body with smooth colourless glaze.

130 (*above right*) John Turner   Floral Pattern (A)
Indented creamware plate (c1806), in medium blue, with floral design on face and moulded border with six small flower sprays.
Impressed mark: TURNER.
Diam 6.8in. Single foot rim. Pale, slightly rippled, greenish-blue glaze on creamware body.

131 (*below*) John Turner
The Villager Pattern (A)
Indented creamware dish (c1825) with moulded border, in medium blue, with six sprays of flowers. The central scene is of villagers—a man, woman and small child, with dog, in a rural setting.
Impressed mark: TURNER 4.
Length 14.2in. Width 12.5in. No foot rim. Very pale blue rippled glaze on creamware body.

Wedgwood Blue-printed Wares

No Wedgwood wares appear to have been printed in underglaze blue in the eighteenth century though the firm was selling creamwares printed over the glaze in black in the 1760s. These were printed in Liverpool by Sadler & Green. S. Shaw in his *History of the Staffordshire Potteries* (1829), p193, tells us that 'the enamellers waited on Mr Wedgwood to solicit his influence in preventing its establishment' and it is understood that he religiously kept his promise not to make blue-printed wares. But in 1795 he died and by the beginning of the nineteenth century Josiah Wedgwood II was firmly established at the helm.

Blue-printed wares were first produced in 1806. The *Chinese Vase Pattern* (133) was the earliest followed by the *Chinese Garden Pattern* (134), almost certainly the pattern referred to as 'Bamboo' in the Wedgwood archives. Both these were based on Chinese originals. Subsequent patterns were mainly floral until John Wedgwood left in 1812. (See Coysh, pp90–94). The *Hibiscus Pattern* which was on sale in 1807 shows the Chinese influence in the border.

All these wares carry the Wedgwood impressed mark. Among the most attractive are the scenes of estuaries and harbours which carry the *Blue Rose* border (136). This border was used on export wares. Laidacker shows it used with a view of Williams College, New England. It was also used by Stevenson & Williams on *Pastoral Scenes* (J. K. des Fontaines, plate 137b).

The design of *The Absalom's Pillar Pattern* (137) was derived, according to Williams (p225), from several engravings in L. Mayer's *Caramanian and Palestine* volumes and has features in common with Spode's *Corinth* pattern. No other similar pattern has been noted from the Wedgwood factory. Williams hazards a guess that 'the engraver who made Spode's copper plates also made this design for Wedgwood at some later date, after he had left the employment of Spode'.

Wedgwood produced earthenware feeding bottles with a *Floral Pattern* (138) probably in the 1830s and 1840s.

There is no doubt that the Wedgwood firm was meticulous about marking the wares. Blue-printed workers' marks are common and so are impressed letters in pairs but they have no value for systematic dating. Year letters were not introduced until 1860. Three-letter impressed marks may be assumed to be after this date.

132 (*above left*) Wedgwood   *Hibiscus Pattern* (A) Plate (c1807–10), in dark blue, with a pattern of hibiscus flowers and leaves radiating from a central medallion. The border design is broken in four places by panels with oriental towers.
Impressed mark: WEDGWOOD (GM 4075).
Printed mark: a small isosceles triangle.
Diam 8in. No foot rim. Clear rippled glaze.

133 (*above right*) Wedgwood
Chinese Vase Pattern (A) Plate (c1806–10), in dark blue, with a Chinese vase showing a seated figure with mandolin. Around it are bamboo trees. The picture is framed in a wide band of 'fret' design. The border is of leaves and flowers.
Impressed mark: WEDGWOOD+
Diam 8.2in. No foot rim. Clear rippled glaze.

134 (*centre left*) Wedgwood
Chinese Garden Pattern (A) Plate (c1806–10), in medium blue, with a fenced-in garden with peonies and bamboos within a Chinese landscape. The border has grape and vine leaf, Chinese writing scroll and flowering thorn motifs.
Impressed mark: WEDGWOOD 44.
Diam 9.6in. No foot rim. Clear glaze on bone china.

135 (*centre right*) Wedgwood
Chinoiserie Willow Pattern (A) Saucer-dish (c1818–20) of bone china, in medium blue, with a Chinese scene of a willow tree, a two-arch bridge, pagodas and a man on a pagoda terrace dangling a bird in a ring from a stick. The border has scroll motifs. The rim is gilded over the glaze.
Printed mark: WEDGWOOD.
Diam 7.1in. Single foot rim. Thick clear glaze on bone china.

136 (*below left*) Wedgwood
Landscape Series (A) *Sicilian Pattern* (A) Indented dished plate (c1835), in dark-medium blue with a harbour scene in Sicily. The Blue Rose border has a stippled ground.
Impressed mark: WEDGWOOD.
Diam 9.9in. No foot rim. Colourless glaze.

137 (*below right*) Wedgwood
'Absalom's Pillar' Pattern Plate (c1822–5), in medium blue, with a Greek scene showing Absalom's Tower. Crocus border.
Impressed mark: WEDGWOOD 33.
Printed mark: three parallel lines with dots.
Diam 9.7in. No foot rim. Clear rippled glaze.

Wood & Challinor of Tunstall

The partnership of John Wood and Edward Challinor came into being in 1828 at Brownhills Pottery, Tunstall. By 1835 they were operating a new factory, the Woodlands Pottery, which continued until 1843. Brownhills Pottery closed in 1841. The wares of this firm are typical of the period of decline in blue-printed wares. They are well made with a good smooth colourless glaze but the designs lack originality. Plates of still poorer quality with the *Corsica* pattern linked with the initials EC were made by Edward Challinor at the Pinnocks Works, Tunstall, after 1842.

Enoch Wood & Sons of Burslem

There were nearly as many potters in the Wood family as in the Adams family but the name of Enoch Wood is the most noteworthy as far as blue-printed wares are concerned. He was among the first of the Staffordshire potters to build up a thriving export trade to America, and Moore lists some 58 American views, over 80 English views and 11 French views among those collected in the USA. One service was produced to mark the opening of the Erie Canal in 1825 (see GI, plate 638).

All the Wood wares were printed in dark blue and many have borders with shells, or shells and flowers. In some cases the picture is circular, in others the border pattern encroaches on the picture to form an irregular dark blue frame. A series of London views included scenes in Regent's Park, and the Bank of England (Little, plate 77). Country views include scenes with abbeys, castles and historic houses. Some of the engravings for these were based on those in John Preston Neale's *Views of the Seats of the Noblemen in England, Wales, Scotland and Ireland* (1818–23) and others on aquatints engraved by John Hunt after George Webster, published by Webster Barrow of 21 White Lion Street, Pentonville, in 1806. The following examples were noted in a Westcountry inn: Thornton Castle, Staffs; Harewood House, Yorks; Guy's Cliff, Warwickshire (Little, plate 78); Sutton Court, Herefordshire; Wardour Castle, Wilts.

The 'Zoological' or 'Sporting' series was no doubt marketed both in Britain and America. It is printed in dark blue and bears the impressed eagle mark (GM 4257). The series included shooting ducks (140), stags (141), hunter shooting fox; leopard; two whippets; zebra; tiger hunt; polar bear hunt; elephant; moose; wolf; hyena; and pointer and quail (see Laidacker, Part II, p105).

138 (*above left*) Wedgwood   Floral Pattern (A)
Feeding bottle (c1830–40), in medium blue, with sprigs of flowers, the base covered by a single spray.
Impressed mark: WEDGWOOD P.
Length 5.8in. Smooth clear glaze on white moulded body.

139 (*above right*) Wood & Challinor
                                   'Corsica' Pattern
Dished plate (c1830–40), in blue (with a violet tinge), with a classical scene. The figures are in seventeenth-century costume. An elaborate border with six bands of geometrical and scroll decoration is broken by four panels with classical buildings or baskets of flowers.
Printed mark: The Staffordshire Knot with W. & C. within the loops. Above this is a rectangular panel with the word CORSICA surmounted by an urn and sprays of flowers.
Diam 10.5in. Rounded foot rim. Clear smooth glaze.

140 (*below left*) Enoch Wood & Sons
                                   Sporting Series (A)
                            Shooting Ducks Pattern (A)
(*Courtesy: Mr and Mrs Graham Salmon*)
Indented plate (c1820), in dark blue, with a country scene showing a man shooting wild geese; in the foreground is a retriever dog. The picture is framed by a wavy white line, and the wide border which descends to the face of the plate consists of floral sprays and scrolls against a cellular or net background.
Impressed mark: ENOCH WOOD & SONS BURSLEM curved round an eagle (GM 4257).
Diam 9.8in. Single foot rim. Rippled blue glaze.

141 (*below right*) Enoch Wood & Sons
                  Sporting Series (A) Stags Pattern (A)
(*Courtesy: Mr and Mrs Graham Salmon*)
Indented plate (c1820), in dark blue, with a parkland scene with two stags. The picture is framed by a wavy white line, and the wide border which descends to the face of the plate consists of floral sprays and scrolls against a cellular or net background.
Impressed mark: as on 140.
Diam 9.8in. Single foot rim. Rippled blue glaze.

PROBLEMS OF ATTRIBUTION

Ceramic Archaeology

Ceramic archaeology involves the careful excavation of old pottery sites and a study of the 'wasters' or 'shards' recovered from the factory tips. When these are compared with unmarked pieces many new facts are revealed. The knowledge of Worcester and Caughley porcelains has been enormously increased by these methods of research.

Excavation of the old site of the Islington Pottery in Liverpool which was operated by Mason, Wolfe & Lucock (c1795–1800) revealed shards with patterns which correspond with those on existing complete pieces (142). This makes accurate attribution possible. However, there are few old sites available today for excavation and other less reliable methods must be used.

Ceramic Marks

Little blue-printed earthenware has been faked, though a few copies of sought-after patterns by James and Ralph Clews did appear on the market a few years ago. Nevertheless, some marks should be treated with caution. The jug (143) which bears an open crescent mark was sold as 'Caughley'. The colour is much lighter than the dark steely-blue characteristic of most Caughley earthenwares and much stipple has been used in the engraving of the unidentified one-man chinoiserie pattern. No other Caughley earthenware has been noted with stipple engraving which only came in well after 1800. Yet ceramic archaeology has proved that porcelain teawares in the medium blue were made at Caughley until 1815. Were earthenwares also made at this period? One can only give the verdict: possibly Caughley, because there is some doubt and one cannot entirely trust the mark.

The small plate (144) which bears an impressed 'S' was also sold as 'Salopian'. There is even more doubt about this attribution. There is no evidence that floral borders of this kind were used by Caughley. The mark may not represent a maker's name at all. If it does, the maker is more likely to be John Shorthose of Hanley (1807–23). Verdict: possibly Shorthose.

The knife-rests (145) raise a different point. They are clearly marked MORTLOCK and the inexperienced may assume this to be the name of the maker. It is not. A number of wholesale and retail mer-

142 (*above left*) *Mason, Wolfe & Lucock*
Early Chinoiserie Pattern (A)
(*Courtesy: City of Liverpool Museum*)
Tea bowl (c1795–1800), *in dark blue, with chinoiserie, with a 'waster' excavated from the site of the Islington Pottery at Liverpool.*

143 (*above right*) *Possibly Caughley*
One-man Chinoiserie Pattern (A)
Jug (c1810–20), *in medium blue, with a scene with pagodas, trees, a sailing boat, and a single-arch bridge on which there is one man facing to the right. The border is of geometrical motifs and scrolls.*
Printed mark: an open crescent.
Height 3.8in. Narrow flattened foot rim. Greenish-blue glaze.

144 (*below left*) *Possibly John Shorthose*
Bridge and Tower Pattern (A)
Small plate (c1820), *in medium blue, with a view of a single-arch bridge (with tower) over a river or canal. A sailing boat is seen through the arch of the bridge. The border is of flowers and dark leaves against a fine key-pattern ground.*
Impressed mark: S.
Diam 4.2in. Three sets of three stilt marks on base. Smooth blue glaze.

145 (*below right*) *Probably Adams   Tendril* (A)
Pair of knife rests (c1820–5), *in medium blue, with a pattern of stylised flowers and scrolls.*
Impressed mark: MORTLOCK.

chants asked that their name should appear on the wares they sold. Mortlock is the name of a china retailer. William and John Mortlock had premises at 200 Oxford Street and 26 Regent Street, London in the 1820s and kept their Oxford Street shop during the whole of the nineteenth century.

Sometimes printed marks on earthenware give information about patterns or the type of body without giving makers' names. Several times plates with *The Fountain Pattern* (146) have been noted bearing the printed mark SEMI-CHINA WARRANTED. Then, unexpectedly, one turned up with the additional word HIGGINBOTHAM'S. This was Thomas Higginbotham, a 'china and delf seller' in Dublin. *The Fountain Pattern* has now been attributed to C. J. Mason & Co (See Coysh, p46). Marked examples have been reported by Mr G. A. Godden.

The plate with flowers and exotic birds (147) bears a printed mark 'Barker' beneath a cartouche with the pattern name *'Floral Scenery'*. No book of ceramic marks gives this printed name alone, only the impressed mark BARKER, and the firm that used this mark operated c1800. Everything about the plate, however, suggests a later date of manufacture—c1830–45. It may have been made at the Don Pottery which was taken over by Samuel Barker & Son c1834, a firm which used the name BARKER (GM 261).

The plate with the oak leaf and acorn border (148) has two marks but bears no maker's name. One mark is an impressed crown; the other is a printed crown above the pattern title *Dalguise, Perthshire*. The mark cannot be identified from any book of marks, and border patterns cannot be trusted though they sometimes give a clue. The oak leaf and acorn border was used by Ralph Stevenson (1810–25) and also by Ralph Stevenson & Williams 1825–32 (GI, plate 549) on export wares to America. Dalguise, Perthshire is not recorded as one of Stevenson's views. It was a pattern used by Enoch Wood, but with a border of grapevines with fruit and flowers. However, both Stevenson and Wood used material from Neale's *The Seats of The Noblemen of England, Wales, Scotland and Ireland* (1818–23). Verdict: possibly Ralph Stevenson.

A dish (149), superbly decorated with a view similar to the 'scene after Claude Lorraine' used by Leeds and J. & R. Riley (pp44–5), bears the printed words: SEMI CHINA enclosed in an eight-sided panel with pseudo-Chinese characters.

This mark has not been identified nor has the

146 *(above left) Attributed to C. J. Mason & Co.*
The Fountain Pattern (A)
Indented plate (c1826–30), in medium blue, with a parkland scene with figures. There is a large country mansion and an elaborate fountain in the foreground with mythological beasts and a man with a club attacking a many-headed dragon-like creature. Deer rest beneath the trees. The border of flowers and leaves on a stipple ground is divided into eight parts by cusped motifs which point inwards.
Impressed mark: a small diamond.
Printed mark: HIGGINBOTHAM'S SEMI-CHINA WARRANTED—*in three lines.*
Diam 10in. Rounded foot rim. Thick blue glaze.

147 *(above right) Possibly Don Pottery*
'Floral Scenery' Pattern
Dished indented plate (c1840) with moulded border, in pale blue, with a scene set among flowers and trees. There is a stone urn of flowers, exotic birds with long tails in a tree, and a passionflower in the foreground. The border is of flowers and C-scrolls.
Printed mark: FLORAL SCENERY *in a cartouche with 'Barker' beneath.*
Diam 10.5in. Rounded foot rim. Smooth blue glaze.

148 *(below left) Possibly Ralph Stevenson*
'Dalguise, Perthshire'
Indented plate (c1810–25), in medium blue, with a view of Dalguise, Perthshire. There are many figures in the park which has a river and a bridge. Two men are fishing; a woman walks with a child and dog, a basket over her arm. The border is of acorns and oak leaves on a fine net ground.
Impressed mark: a crown.
Printed mark: 'Dalguise, Perthshire' in an eight-sided panel surmounted by a crown. Conifer sprays decorate the sides.
Diam 10in. Double foot rim. Rippled blue glaze.

149 *(below right) Unknown Maker*
Italian Ruins Pattern (A)
Vegetable dish (c1810–25), in medium blue, with a scene with ruins, a river and a three-arch bridge. The wide border of trailing hops and barley ears has a cellular or fine net ground.
Printed mark: SEMI-CHINA *in an eight-sided panel with a pseudo-Chinese border (Little, fig 105) and a small clover-leaf mark.*
Diam 9.5in. Flattened foot rim. Rippled blue glaze.

charming border of hops and barley ears. The net background is similar to that used on some pieces by Clews (pp22 and 24). The tiny clover-leaf workman's mark was used on Cambrian Pottery wares (GM 3763). A small but similar mark with the words SEMI-CHINA in a rectangle has been noted on a jug by Rheuben Johnson of Hanley made for the coronation of George IV in 1821. Nevertheless, the only possible verdict is: maker unknown.

Doubtful Attributions

In view of the lack of supporting evidence it is sometimes necessary to question the attributions made by some museum curators and earlier writers, not in any carping way but in the hope that hitherto unknown facts may be brought to light.

The Village Church Pattern on an unmarked plate is attributed by Little (plate 72) to Wedgwood of Etruria, but without comment except that he regards it as typical of Wedgwood's rustic patterns. The same pattern on an unmarked plate (150) in the author's collection has been compared carefully with a number of Wedgwood plates (132–7) but the body, colour and glaze bear no resemblance to any of these. Moreover, Wedgwood usually marked his wares. On the other hand dishes have been noted with this pattern, bearing moulded flower handles similar to those used by Rogers (90) and the border pattern corresponds with a border used by Stubbs on export wares. Verdict: possibly Rogers or Stubbs.

The Chinoiserie Pattern (151) has been noted frequently, always unmarked. Williams illustrates an unmarked hot-water plate (fig 106) and expresses the view that it is 'marked all over' as Spode (p147). More definite evidence, however, is now available. J. K. des Fontaines illustrates a plate with this pattern (plate 139d) carrying both impressed and printed Spode marks. One wonders why so many unmarked pieces are to be found from a factory which usually marked its wares. Verdict: almost certainly Spode.

The Greek Pattern (152) is similar to patterns used by Spode (p82) and Herculaneum (see *Transactions of the English Ceramic Circle*, 7, Part I [1968], plate 28b). Williams illustrates a similar plate with a caption 'possibly Pratt' but gives no reasons for his statement. The only factories so far known to have painted the edges of their wares with an ochreous enamel are Swansea and Herculaneum. Verdict: possibly Herculaneum.

The Grazing Rabbits Pattern (153) is a common

150 *(above left) Possibly Rogers or Stubbs*
Village Church Pattern (A)
Indented plate (c1820–35), in medium blue, with a village scene showing a church with tower, cottages, sheep, and two men talking by an open gate. The border is of roses and other flowers on a stipple ground.
Printed mark: Mars mark (circle with an arrow).
Diam 9.8in. No foot rim. Pale blue rippled glaze.

151 *(above right) Almost certainly Spode*
Forest Landscape or Chinoiserie Pattern (A)
Indented plate (c1810–20), in dark-medium blue, with a Chinese scene of houses, trees and a river or lake. One man is seen in the foreground in a partially covered boat. Geometrical border of insects in medallions.
Unmarked.
Diam 9.4in. No foot rim. Smooth colourless glaze.

152 *(below left) Possibly Herculaneum*
Greek Key-border Pattern
Indented plate (c1810–20), in dark blue, with a classical pattern of chariots and figures around a central floral circle. The key-pattern border carries six medallions with figures on a stipple ground. The edge of the plate is painted a yellow-ochre colour over the glaze.
Unmarked.
Diam 8in. No foot rim. Pale greenish-blue rippled glaze.

153 *(below right) Unknown Maker*
'The Grazing Rabbits' Pattern
Indented plate (c1820), in medium blue, with a country scene with cottages and three rabbits under a tree. The border is of flowers and dark leaves against a stipple ground.
Unmarked.
Diam 8in. No foot rim. Three single stilt marks. Pale greenish-blue glaze.

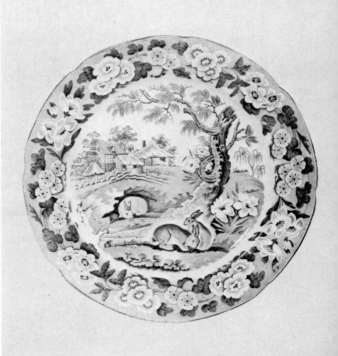

one on dinner wares. A large number of pieces bearing this design have been examined but none has been marked. Yet this pattern is commonly attributed to Rogers. Little gives this attribution, for example (p 94). Why? Rogers & Son seem normally to have marked their wares. Why should so many pieces of this particular pattern be left unmarked? Until a marked specimen is recorded the verdict must be: maker unknown.

The Castle and Bridge Pattern (154), with twisted trees, can be attributed to Henshall & Co, a Staffordshire firm involving a number of partnerships, which appears to have traded under this title from c1795 to c1828. Marked specimens have been recorded.

The Bee Master Pattern, printed on a tureen stand (155) in dark blue, is extremely attractive and might be described as a rural conversation piece. A dish with this design was illustrated in an issue of *Country Life* (25 January 1968, p168). An American correspondent writing from a farm at Wading River, New York, said: 'We think it is Adams' but asked for confirmation. The reply to his letter included the following statement:

> The animal medallions and flower motifs composing the border of this dish form a design that has been seen on wares made by W. Adams & Sons, who operated at Greengates, Staffordshire, from 1819-1864; the design was also continued by their successors. This border is not known to have been used before the early 1830s. The design is one of a series of English Countryside views and is known as 'The Bee Master'. Adams produced transfers of this kind in red, blue and green during the 1830s but examination of ceramic, glaze and form of the dish would be necessary before one could attribute this piece with certainty. All the successful potters had their wares copied by lesser firms.

An examination of this tureen stand suggests an earlier date than 1830. It may well have been included among export wares soon after William Adams went to America in 1821 to promote his business. The Colombus Views he made for export bear a border of 'medallions, animals and flowers' though it is not identical with that on the *Bee Master* pieces. Verdict: possibly Adams.

154 (*above*) *Henshall & Co*
  Castle and Bridge Pattern (A) *Dish* (c1810–28) *with wavy edge, in medium blue, with a scene of a castle on a hill, a four-arch bridge, houses, and fishermen in a boat with a net. The branches of the trees are distorted. The border has trees, a church, a cottage and ruins.*
Unmarked.
Length 12.8in. Width 9.8in. No foot rim. Pale blue slightly rippled glaze.

155 (*below*) *Possibly Adams*
  'The Bee Master' Pattern Tureen stand (c1825), *in dark-medium blue, with a country scene with a church on a hill, and cottages. Figures and dogs occupy the foreground. A beekeeper with sleeves rolled up carries a beehive. The picture is framed in a scrolled band. The border of flowers against a stipple ground carries eight medallions with views of horses, stags, cows and sheep. The moulded handles carry small circles on a cellular or net ground.*
Unmarked.
Length 15in. Width 9.5in. No well-defined foot rim. Clear smooth glaze.

Patterns and Shapes

The pattern on an unmarked piece of blue-printed ware is only a clue to a possible maker; it does not necessarily lead to a certain attribution. In the same way decorative shapes can sometimes give a clue to a likely maker. The oval dish (156) has mark, pattern and shape but even these three clues do not lead to certain attribution. The mark (157) does not bear the maker's name nor can it be traced in any books of marks. The shape of the dish has not been noted on any marked pieces. The pattern, however, has a special interest. It has the same double printing which was noted on a decorative comport by Rogers (90): the distant scene in light blue, the foreground in dark blue. The author was able to examine a large 'English Scenery' service. It included five distinct views, all with a background of ancient buildings and a foreground with water and a sailing boat. One of these used the identical building from the Rogers comport (90) for its background. Moreover the smooth white finish is similar to late pieces (after c1830) made by this firm. Verdict: almost certainly Rogers.

The dish with the cusped edge (158) is unmarked. The shape, however, is one that was used by Spode though the illustrated example by Williams (fig 84) has cusps that are a little more rounded. The pattern is the well known Spode's *Gothic Castle*. However, many unmarked examples with this pattern have been noted and J. & B. Baddeley made dishes of the same shape (GI 22). Verdict: probably Spode.

The square dish (159) with cusped edge has a quatrefoil pattern printed in dark blue. This shape was used by Spode, though perhaps not exclusively. J. K. des Fontaines illustrates a plate with this quatrefoil pattern with the impressed and printed mark of Spode (plate 141b). He considers that this may be *The Persian Pattern* referred to by L. Jewitt in *The Ceramic Art of Great Britain* (1883). Unfortunately Williams and the Spode factory have used the same title for a later border pattern (Williams, fig 147). The pattern illustrated (159) has therefore been called *The Persian Quatrefoil Pattern* to avoid confusion. Verdict: probably Spode.

Coffee pots, small jugs and creamers usually present a special problem since marked pieces in these forms do not appear very often. Four unmarked examples are shown on p107 and so far it has been impossible to attribute them definitely to their respective makers.

The coffee pot (160) was sold by discerning

NOTE. *View page 105 from outer edge*

156 (*above left*) Almost certainly Rogers
'English Scenery' Pattern
Oval indented dish (c1825–40), in medium blue, with a sailing boat on river or lake. A Tudor house in a setting of trees forms a pale blue background. The border of small flowers is repeated below the rim.
Printed mark: see 157.
Length 10.4in. Width 7.2in. Flattened foot rim. Smooth colourless glaze.

157 (*above right*) Almost certainly Rogers
'English Scenery' Pattern
Printed mark on base of dish (156) with SEMI-CHINA *on a draped scroll above the words* ENGLISH SCENERY, *the whole surmounted by a crown.*

158 (*below left*) Probably Spode
'Gothic Castle' Pattern
Dish (c1810–20) with cusped edge, in medium blue, with chinoiserie including trees, a bridge and a vase of flowers, in which setting appears a gothic castle and some 'ruins of uncertain character'. The border is geometrical with medallions with animals including elephant, giraffe and deer.
Unmarked.
Length 9.8in. Width 7in. Flattened foot rim. Greenish-blue glaze.

159 (*below right*) Probably Spode
'Flower Cross' or Persian Quatrefoil Pattern (A)
Dish (1810–20) with cusped edge, in dark blue, with a symmetrical design of four flower or leaf motifs separated by trailing flowers. The border is of dark flowers and leaves against a geometrical ground. The design is of fine line engraving.
Unmarked.
Length of diagonal 9in. Flattened foot rim. Rippled blue glaze.

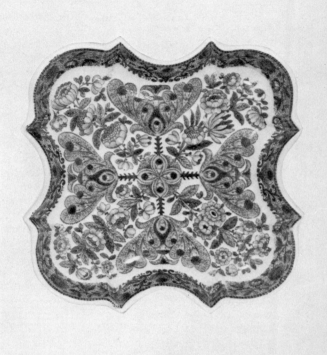

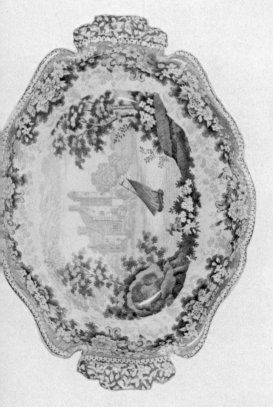

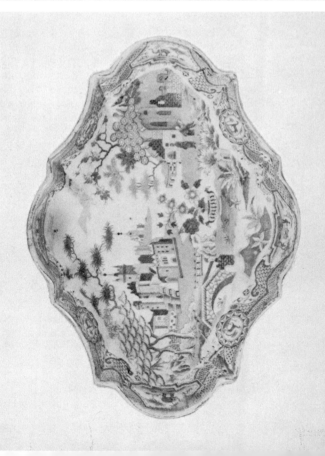

dealers who are also collectors. They attributed it to 'Liverpool' because of the shape of the handle. They had accumulated a large series of photographs of pieces that had passed through their hands and the attribution was based on a study of shapes. Unfortunately no marked pieces with this shape or with this *Chinese Raft Pattern* have been recorded.

The knop on the lid, which is moulded as a fleur-de-lys, is similar to a knop on the cover of a basalt sugar made by John Warburton of Cobridge between 1802 and 1823 (GI, plate 593) though they are not identical. A Liverpool Museum authority tells me that he agrees with the attribution of the vendors, basing his view on 'the shape of the handle' and on a porcelain teapot 'with the same shaped knop' which he firmly believes to be Herculaneum.

The jug with the lion spout (161) is clearly a late piece of blue-printed ware. The rococo motifs in the pattern are typical of the 1830s and it has a smooth clear glaze. Although the shape is unusual it is believed that more than one potter produced jugs and teapots with lion spouts. Several examples, however, have been noted with the mark of Elijah Mayer & Son of Cobden Works, Hanley. Bevis Hillier in his *Pottery and Porcelain, 1700–1914* (1968) illustrates a basalt teapot of this type (plate 154) by this maker, c1830. Verdict: possibly Elijah Mayer & Son.

The jug with the royal arms (162) bears some resemblance to another jug with the royal arms printed beneath the lip (GI 21) but does not carry the same pattern. Godden attributes his example, which is marked 'B & B', 'possibly' to Baggerley & Ball. However, as this firm closed down before Queen Victoria came to the throne its products would not have carried the Victorian royal arms. An appendix note on B & B (GM 4405a) refers to firms which might have used these initials with the royal arms. They include Beardmore & Birks of Longton (c1831–43); Bailey & Ball of Longton (c1843–50); and Bridgwood & Burgess of Longton (c1846–7). There is no clue on the jug illustrated here (162) to lead to an attribution.

The cup (163) presents an interesting problem. At first it seems that there are no clues. The glaze, however, has a 'gritty' quality only seen on plates by Hamilton of Stoke (47 and 48). On examining the pieces together it is seen that the colours are identical, the use of combined line and stipple engraving is similar and even the style of design, particularly the heads of the animals (with prominent nostrils) is similar. Verdict: possibly Hamilton of Stoke.

160 (*above left*) *probably Herculaneum*
            Chinese Raft Pattern (A)
Coffee pot (c1810), in dark-medium blue, with a Chinese scene with mountains, trees, domed buildings and figures. The prominent feature is a raft propelled on the river by a boy. The borders repeat the features of the picture—mountains, trees, buildings and the raft. The lower part of the coffee pot is moulded with 'basket weave'; the knop of the lid is shaped like the fleur-de-lys.
Unmarked.
Height 9.5in from base to knop. Shallow flattened foot rim. Greenish-blue glaze on cream-coloured body.

161 (*above right*) *Possibly E. Mayer & Son*
             Fruit-table Pattern (A)
Jug (c1840) with a lion's head spout, in pale blue, with fruit and flowers trailing over a table. The border of C-scrolls is also decorated with fruit and flowers and is repeated inside the rim. A C-scroll design decorates the handle.
Impressed mark: k.
Height 5in from base to spout. Rounded foot rim. Smooth colourless glaze.

162 (*below left*) *Unknown Maker*
             Victorian Armorial Pattern (A)
Jug (c1840), in dark-medium blue, with a maritime scene showing a young man with a book seated beside a girl holding a lyre. Below the spout is the Victorian royal coat of arms. The border has small flowers, leaves and scrolls.
Unmarked.
Height 5in. Foot rim. Clear smooth glaze.

163 (*below right*) *Possibly Hamilton*
             Deer Pattern (A)
Cup (c1820), in dark blue, with a scene of deer in fields and woodland. The border pattern inside the cup is of stylised flowers and leaves, alternating. Inside the cup, at the bottom, is a print of a single deer.
Unmarked.
Diam at rim 4.1in. Height 2.7in. Deep foot rim. Thick gritty blue glaze.

Makers Unknown

The remaining illustrations in this book are of pieces which yield few clues likely to lead to definite attribution.

The Gleaners Pattern (164) shows the finest engraving and transfer printing the author has ever seen. It must certainly have been produced by a firm with highly skilled and experienced workers. Although it does not carry the same border it bears a remarkable similarity to a plate in a 'British Views' series which has the rare impressed mark of Henshall & Co of Longport (Little, plate 34). The flowers in the borders are similar and both borders have bunches of fruit, all against a stipple ground. In both cases the border is wide, extending into the well of the plate where it is separated from the central picture by stringing.

In a valuable account of this firm which apparently engaged in the export trade to America, Little expresses the view that it 'took a more important part in the production of underglaze blue transfer-printed wares than has hitherto been recognized'. Any collector who may possess specimens with the mark of Henshall & Co should have them photographed and publish details. More clear evidence is needed about many of the lesser known makers of these blue and white wares.

The Spotted Deer Pattern (165) should be compared with Rogers' *Zebra Pattern* (80) or, better still, the Toft & May version (Little, plate 67). The buildings show some similarities. Verdict: maker unknown.

The Eastern Port Pattern (166) with the crowns in the border and the Union Jack panel in the fence gives no clues. Verdict: maker unknown.

The Bamboo and Flower Pattern (167) has features in common with Davenport's *Bamboo and Peony Pattern* (29) and Wedgwood's *Chinese Garden Pattern* (134). It bears the SEMI-CHINA mark (Little, fig 105) seen also on a vegetable dish (149). Verdict: maker unknown.

The Octagonal Chinoiserie Pattern (168) provides no clue though the castle reminds one of Spode's *Gothic Castle* (158). Verdict: maker unknown.

The Pashkov Palace Pattern (169) could well have been made for export to Russia. The Pashkov Palace in Moscow was built in 1784 and later became the Rumyanstev Museum. Verdict: maker unknown.

The author would be glad to hear from anyone who may have traced marked pieces with these unattributed patterns.

164 (*above left*)   *The Gleaners Pattern* (A) Dished indented plate (c1810–20), in dark-medium blue, with a scene with two women holding bundles of corn and a girl fondling a dog. Border of flowers, fruit and large scrolls against a stipple ground. Impressed mark: 17. Diam 9.5in. Double foot rim. Greenish-blue rippled glaze.

165 (*above right*)   *'Spotted Deer' Pattern* Indented plate (c1810–20), in dark-medium blue, showing buildings, and trees with splayed boles. There are two spotted deer, one standing, one resting. Border has a number of geometrical motifs, each repeated four times. Unmarked. Diam 9½in. No foot rim. Greenish-blue rippled glaze.

166 (*centre left*)   *Eastern Port Pattern* (A) Indented plate (c1810–30), in a soft medium blue, with a scene in an eastern port. There are anchored ships with sails furled, minarets, domed buildings and clouds of smoke surround a table. A standing figure holds a long-stemmed pipe, a horseman holds a lance. The border of flowers bears four crowns. Unmarked. Diam 9.8in. No foot rim. Greenish-blue glaze.

167 (*centre right*) *Bamboo and Flower Pattern* (A) Indented plate (c1810–30), in dark-medium blue, with bamboo and flowers, some in a vase. The border is of scrolls and flowers. Impressed mark: 7. Printed mark: SEMI-CHINA as in 149. Diam 9.9in. Double foot rim. Rippled blue glaze.

168 (*below left*) *Octagonal Chinoiserie Pattern* (A) Indented plate (c1810–25), in dark blue, with an octagonal picture of a building (with castle and pagoda elements). A man stands at a table with a jug, a small child holds a plate, and a lady with crown and trident is seated before them. The border has eight eight-sided medallions alternately with flowers and dog with figures. The ground of the plate has a geometrical pattern. Unmarked. Diam 10in. Single foot rim. Thick blue rippled glaze, unevenly applied.

169 (*below right*)   *'The Pashkov Palace' Pattern* Indented plate (c1810–25), in medium blue, with a view of the Pashkov Palace, Moscow. The border of flowers has a stippled ground. Unmarked. Diam 8in. Single foot rim. Greenish-blue glaze.

NOTES FOR THE COLLECTOR

It may encourage the new collector of blue and white transfer-printed earthenware to know that of the pieces illustrated in this book most are in the collection made by the author over a period of five years. There are still pieces to be found, sometimes quite cheaply, though the wares are not so readily come by as they were some years ago and prices are rising. One now looks more and more for quality in the engraving and transfer work and, above all, one likes to see a maker's mark. But an unmarked piece of fine quality such as the coffee pot (160) is infinitely preferable to a marked piece of poor quality such as the Godwin plate (44), though some poor quality pieces have a special interest (18).

When examining a piece with a view to purchase:

(i) Decide first whether it has 'quality'.

(ii) Hold the piece so that the light is reflected from the surface. Early wares before about 1820 usually have a fine ripple in the glaze; in later pieces the glaze is usually smooth.

(iii) Note the colour of the glaze, especially where it may have run against a foot rim. Early glazes have a strong tinge of blue or sometimes green.

(iv) Look for signs of wear. Many early plates and dishes have no foot rim. Natural wear on the glaze resulting from years of use are some indication of age. Dishes particularly have often suffered wear from being pushed about on stone slabs of Victorian pantries.

(v) Look for the spur or stilt marks on the base (and sometimes the face) of a plate where the wares were supported on small pyramids of baked clay in the kilns.

(vii) Do not assume that you can attribute an unmarked plate to a maker simply because it carries a border he is known to have used.

The last illustrations in this book show the contrasting results which can be obtained by the combined use of line and stipple engraving. *The Village Fishermen Pattern* (170) is crisp and well defined, yet a good perspective is achieved. This strainer is unmarked but was acquired for its quality. Since then an American collector has reported a plate with this pattern impressed J. & W. Handley. This firm appears to have potted at the Albion Works, Hanley, from c1802–c1828. *The Italian Pastoral Pattern* (171) has something of the soft dreamy quality of a Claude Lorraine painting. Surely the finest blue-printed wares must be regarded as co-operative works of art?

170 (above)   *Attributed to J. & W. Handley*
Village Fishermen Pattern (A)
Dish strainer (c1815–28), in medium blue, with river scene showing a six-arched bridge, village church and distant hills. Two fishermen stand in the water and there are three cows in the foreground. There is a narrow border with a fleur-de-lys motif.
Unmarked.
Length 12.8in. Width 9.2in. Pale blue glaze on slightly cream-coloured body.

171 (below) *Unknown maker*
Italian Pastoral Pattern (A)
Dish strainer (c1815–30), in medium blue, with an Italian river scene of a five-arch bridge and a building with tower. A large tree dominates the scene which has cattle, goats and figures in the foreground. There is no border.
Impressed mark: N and 16.
Length 13.3in. Width 9.2in. Smooth pale blue glaze.

INDEX

(*Numbers refer to pages*)

Abbey, Richard, 18
Adams, William, 10, 20, 21, 102-3
Alcock, Samuel, 20, 21
Ainsworth, John, 16

Baddeley, William, 78
Baggerley & Ball, 106
Baker, Bevans & Irwin, 78, 88, 89, 90, 91
Barker, Samuel & Son, 32, 48, 98
Bell, J. & M. P. & Co, 48
Bevington, T. & J., 78, 88
Bourne, Baker & Bourne, 48
Bovey Tracey Pottery, 48
Boyle, Zachariah, 76
Brameld, William, 60, 61
Bristol Pottery, 50-4

Cambrian Pottery, 16, 17, 18, 88, 89, 90
Carey, Thomas, 20, 21, 22, 23
Carey, John, 20, 21, 22, 23
Carr, John, 26
Carr & Patten, 26
Case, Thomas, 18
Castleford Pottery, 16
Caughley Pottery, 7, 10, 11, 14, 96
Clews, James, 22, 23, 24, 25, 78, 96
Clews, Ralph, 22, 23, 24, 25, 78, 96
Coalport Works, 24, 25
Cornfoot, Colville & Co, 26, 27

Davenport, John, 16, 26, 27, 28, 29, 30, 31, 32, 33
Dillwyn, Lewis Weston, 78, 88, 89, 90
Donovan, 78, 98
Don Pottery, 16, 32, 33, 34, 35, 48
Du Croz, John, 42, 43
Dunderdale, David, 16

Elkins & Co, 34, 35
Elkin, Knight & Co, 34
Elkin, Knight & Bridgwood, 34, 35, 36, 37

Fell, Thomas, 36, 37, 38, 39
Fell & Co, 36, 37, 48
Foley Pottery (Fenton), 34, 35
Glamorgan Pottery, 78, 88, 89, 90, 91

Godwin, Thomas, 38, 39
Godwin, Benjamin, 38, 39

Hall, John, 38
Hall, Ralph, 38, 39
Hamilton, Robert, 40, 41, 106, 107
Hartley, Greens & Co, 44
Heath, Joshua, 10, 11, 12, 13, 14, 15, 16
Heathcote, Charles & Co, 40, 41
Henshall & Co, 102, 108
Herculaneum Pottery, 18, 19, 42, 43, 66, 82, 100, 106, 107
Hicks & Meigh, 42, 43
Hicks, Meigh & Johnson, 42, 43
Higginbotham, 98

Islington Pottery, 18, 44, 96-7

Jones & Son (Hanley), 44, 45

Knight, Elkin & Co, 34
Knight, Elkin & Bridgwood, 34-7

Leeds Pottery, 16, 17, 18, 44, 45, 98
Lucas, Thomas, 16
Lucock, John, 44

Maddock & Seddon, 50, 51
Mare, John, 76
Mason, G. M. & C. J., 16, 46, 47
Mason, Miles, 44, 45
Mason, Wolfe & Lucock, 96, 97
Mayer, Elijah, 106, 107
Meigh, Charles, 46
Meigh, Job, 46, 47
Meir, John, 48, 49
Meir, John & Son, 48
Middlesbrough Pottery, 48, 49
Minton, Herbert, 50, 51
Minton, Thomas, 10, 18
Mist, James Underhill, 14
Mort, John, 18
Mortlock, 96, 97, 98

Pountney & Allies, 50, 52, 53, 76
Pountney & Goldney, 50, 51, 52, 53, 62, 76
Pratt, F. & R. & Co Ltd, 20

Read, Clementson & Anderson, 48
Richards, James, 16
Ridgway, John & William, 54, 55, 56, 57
Riley, John & Richard, 52, 56, 57, 58, 59, 60, 61
Rockingham Works, 60, 61
Rogers, John & George, 60
Rogers, John & Son, 52, 60, 61, 62, 63, 64, 65, 66, 67, 68, 69, 70, 71, 100, 102, 104, 105, 108
Rothwell, Thomas, 18

Sadler & Green, 92
Shorthose & Co, 70, 71
Shorthose & Heath, 70
Sewell, 78
Shorthose, John, 70, 96
Spode Factory (Stoke), 10, 16, 17, 18, 19, 52, 72, 73, 74, 75, 76, 77, 78, 79, 80, 81, 82, 83, 84, 85, 86, 87, 100, 104, 105
Stevenson, Andrew, 86, 87, 88, 89
Stevenson, Ralph, 86, 98
Stevenson & Williams, 98
Stubbs, Joseph, 88, 100
Stubbs & Kent, 88, 89
Swansea Potteries, 16, 17, 88, 89, 90, 91

Tittensor, Charles, 82
Toft & May, 62, 98, 108
Townsend, George, 48
Turner, John, 10, 14, 15, 16, 40, 90, 91
Turner, Thomas, 7, 10, 14

Underwood, William, 16, 90

Warburton, John, 106
Wedgwood (Etruria), 92, 93, 94, 95, 100
Wolfe, Thomas, 10, 40, 44
Wood, Enoch & Sons, 94, 95, 98
Wood & Challinor, 94, 95
Worthington, Humble & Holland, 18

Yates, John, 10, 16